Life's a Beach

George Mahood

For Doug and Chris

Also by George Mahood

Every Day Is a Holiday:
The hilarious true story of one dad's attempt to celebrate the weird and wonderful calendar days

Free Country:
A Penniless Adventure the Length of Britain

Not Tonight, Josephine:
A Road Trip Through Small-Town America

Travels with Rachel:
In Search of South America

Operation Ironman:
One Man's Four Month Journey from Hospital Bed to Ironman Triathlon

Did Not Finish:
Misadventures in Running, Cycling and Swimming

The Self-Help Bible:
All the Answers for a Happier, Healthier Life

How Not to Get Married:
A no-nonsense guide to weddings, from a photographer who has seen it ALL

JULY

July 1st

I set out at the beginning of January to spend the first half of the year celebrating as many of the bizarre, weird and wonderful 'official' holidays as possible. It was an incredible six months and I learned a lot. Some of it useful. Most of it less so. But it had been a great deal of fun and I was not ready for the experience to end.

On the last day of June (it feels like only yesterday. Oh wait, it was) my wife Rachel suggested that I continue the project for the remaining six months, in order to fully embrace the challenge. I gladly accepted.

The second half of the year promised to be even better than the first. Our house was for sale, a move to Devon was planned, holidays were booked, microadventures were intended, and there would be new schools, new careers and new beginnings. I could not wait to get started.

July 1st is *Second Half of the Year Day* - a day to evaluate the year so far and set new goals. It is a basic concept, but I am surprised it doesn't get more recognition. January 1st obviously takes all of the attention with New Year's resolutions and new starts. But why shouldn't the second half of the year be given equal credit? The temptation is to almost write off making any changes until the end of the year. As soon as people get to July, they start saying *'I can't believe it's July already. Where has the year gone? Hasn't it just flown by.'*

Well, no it hasn't. Time goes at the same speed that it always has. As you grow older, there is a definite feeling that time speeds up. This is because the markers by which we measure our time become further apart. When we are children, every second of every minute counts; we want to fill our every waking moment with some form of excitement or activity. As we grow up and become teenagers, we begin making our own plans - scheduling activities on a day-to-day basis - so our concept of time is altered. We then reach adulthood and our working life begins. The majority of our time is spent working - often in a job we don't enjoy - and time becomes measured by the distance between the things we enjoy, such as the weekends. A year is no longer 365 days; it is just 52 weekends. Weekends then start to fly by, and then months, and before you know it is July 1st, and hasn't the year just flown by?

Rather than reaching July 1st and thinking *'where has the first half of the year gone?'* why not turn it around, and remind yourself that you still have half of the year - that's ONE HUNDRED AND EIGHTY FOUR DAYS - remaining. And it's all irrelevant anyway, because as one year ends, a new one begins, and the whole thing continues as before.

The first half of this holiday challenge had forced me to not focus on the days, weeks, and months. I had filled my time with new experiences and things I enjoyed, and, as a result, the markers by which my time was measured had changed dramatically.

This book was supposed to be a mildly amusing memoir, and it has turned into a deep and philosophical rant on theories of time. That's enough bullshit from me. Let's proceed with the nonsense.

July 3rd

During my time at university I had a little career on the side as a Professional Police Identity Parade Actor. That's not an official title, but it's what I put on my CV. I had heard that you could get paid to appear in police line-ups, so I went to the local police station one morning and registered my details. Leeds is a big city and therefore had plenty of criminals, plenty of police line-ups, and plenty of work for Professional Police Identity Parade Actors like me. Being average height, average build (I wasn't so biggishly built back then) and with brown hair, I matched the description of a large proportion of the criminals of West Yorkshire.

During my time in Leeds I did about three identity parades per week. I was the only student who took part. The others were all decent guys, but self-confessed ex-criminal drug addicts. They were all on first name terms with the policemen from previous, less 'professional' encounters, and they openly talked about going to spend their earnings on drugs. We were paid £8 for a standard line-up - even when they got cancelled, which they often did. If they lasted longer than an hour we got paid overtime. We were paid there and then, in cash, in a little envelope, and we would all walk off in different directions to spend it how we chose. I spent mine on cheap lager - my vice of choice - at the £1-a-pint Student Union, which was somehow morally more acceptable than the drugs bought by the others.

It was an easy way to earn a little extra spending money, and the parades themselves were surprisingly enjoyable. We had to sit or stand in a room, facing a one-way mirror. The suspected criminal was then brought into the room by a police officer and placed in a random seat alongside us. It was very difficult to not spend the entire time looking at the suspect in the mirror. Often the suspect's lawyer would kick up a fuss about the others in the line-up not bearing any resemblance to the accused, and the parade would have to be cancelled.

On two separate occasions I was picked out by the witness. The first time it happened I was terrified; an officer came in and said: 'you were identified in that parade, I hope you've got a good lawyer', before breaking into laughter along with all the others. The second time it happened, I knew the protocol, and laughed along with the rest.

Occasionally we would have to do something different like say a particular phrase, or wear a hat. If the suspect had any notable facial scars or earrings then we would all have to wear plasters in that exact same spot so that the person was not picked out simply because of that one characteristic.

During one line-up, the spotlights came on and a voice over the intercom requested quiet, signifying that the witness was about to appear on the other side of the mirror. We all sat in silence for a few seconds until I caught sight of the suspect, sat a couple of seats away from me, winking at himself in the mirror. He then ran his fingers through his hair, pointed to his reflection and said 'loooking gooood.' He was identified immediately by the witness and escorted out of the room by the policeman.

Today was *Compliment Your Mirror Day*, and every time I have looked at myself in a mirror since, it has reminded me of my career as a Professional Police Identity Parade Actor. Today I looked in the mirror, ran my fingers through my hair, pointed at my reflection and said 'looooking gooood,' before heading to the shop.

It was not until I reached the checkout that I remembered it was *International Plastic Bag Free Day*. I had a small rucksack, but had purchased far more groceries than I intended. Not wanting to set the second half of the year off to a bad start, I packed the rucksack, filled the pockets of my cargo shorts, stuffed several bulky items up my t-shirt and piled the rest precariously into my arms.

'Are you sure you don't want a bag for all that?' asked the cashier.

'Nooo! I'll be fine,' I said defiantly.

I waddled home looking like the Michelin Man.

We have a cupboard bursting with bags-for-life. Each time it is opened, a mountain of them spew out onto the floor and I angrily squeeze them back in before wedging the door closed. Whenever Rachel goes to the supermarket, and forgets to take any reusable bags with her, she decides that it's not eco-friendly to use carrier bags, so buys several bags-for-life instead. This happens every single time she goes shopping.

I have tried to point out to Rachel that bags-for-life are only more eco-friendly if they are reused regularly, but she just can't resist.

International Plastic Bag Free Day forms the focus of a push from environmental groups to achieve a ban across Europe on single-use plastic bags. I think it is a great idea and Rachel has inadvertently created a way to make this possible. If there was a worldwide ban on carrier bags today, we could hand our supply of bags-for-life out, and most of the world's population would have a bag. For life.

July 4th

Fourth of July, or *Independence Day*, is one of the most recognised federal holidays in the United States. It commemorates the date in 1776 when the Declaration of Independence was signed, announcing independence from the British Empire.

I celebrated with the worst barbecue I have ever eaten. It was *National Barbecued Spareribs Day*, but those killjoys from *The Vegetarian Awareness Network* designated July 4th *Independence From Meat Day*, too.

Undeterred, and focussed on the challenge, I set about making some vegetarian spare ribs from recipe I found online, using a bunch of peculiar ingredients (gluten, nutritional yeast, onion powder, LIQUID SMOKE?). The result was a revolting, ugly gloop, with the texture of wet cake.

To make it even less appetising, I served the horrendous concoction with an egg that I attempted to cook on the pavement. It was *Sidewalk Egg Frying Day*. Frying eggs on a pavement in England, on an overcast day, is physically impossible. Thankfully, we hadn't invited any guests to our barbecue, and when I say 'we', I mean 'I'. This was a holiday I celebrated alone.

Three consecutive US Presidents (two of whom signed the Declaration of Independence) all died coincidently on 4th July. John Adams and Thomas Jefferson both died on the 50th anniversary of the declaration in 1826, and James Munroe died five years later on 4th July, 1831. Rumours that they died of food poisoning from vegetarian spareribs and sidewalk fried eggs are unsubstantiated.

July 6th

When I was 12 we stayed with my uncle who lived just north of San Francisco in California. He owned a ranch, but his house at the time was made from a large empty wine vat, but that is another story. There was a pond on his ranch, which also doubled as a swimming pool, and it was around this pond that we ate our evening meals, cooked on an open fire. One evening, out of the blue, my uncle suggested that we have a cherry pit spitting contest. We took it in turns to spit the cherry pits across the pond to see who could project them the furthest.

I went first; slobbering a pathetic attempt that barely left my mouth, and sent globules of saliva further than the actual pit. My mum and sister made equally disappointing attempts, before my dad recorded a respectable distance of about six feet. My uncle then stepped up to the edge of the water, tilted his head back and fairly effortlessly spat the cherry pit almost the entire length of the pond - a distance of nearly 30 feet. We watched in amazement as the ripples receded.

'How did you do that?' I asked.

'It must have just been a fluke,' he said coolly.

We all tried again, this time with slightly more success than before, but still not even reaching a quarter of the way across the pond. My uncle tried again, this time matching his previous distance almost exactly.

'Have another go,' I said. 'We need to study your technique.'

This time, his cherry pit cleared the pond, and we faintly heard it fall onto the stones on the other side.

'That was incredible,' I said. 'What's your secret?'

'You have to roll up your tongue tightly, and then blow the pit through your tongue in a short, sharp blow, so that it acts like a peashooter.'

Of course! This technique made perfect sense. How naive of me to just spit it like an amateur. I tried the new technique and the pit sailed through the air, but only slightly further than my previous attempts, and still well short of the halfway point in the pond. The rest of my family were similarly useless.

Everyone else retired back to the campfire and admitted defeat, but I spent the next half an hour trying to perfect my technique, before eventually giving up when I knew I was never going to be able to compete. It was clear that we were no match for my uncle, and we all congratulated him on his extraordinary talent.

A month or so after we got home to England, we received the following letter.

Dear Mahoods,

It was lovely to have you all to stay last month. Thank you so much for making the trip over to California to see us.

There is something that has been playing on my mind since your visit. You will no doubt remember our cherry pit spitting contest at the pond, and how you all marvelled at my spitting ability. Well, I have a confession to make. The technique that I used may breach some of the official cherry pit spitting guidelines. In other words, I'm afraid to say that I cheated. I was actually squeezing the cherry pit between my thumb and forefinger, down by my side, and firing it across the pond at the same time as pretending to spit. I didn't even have a cherry pit in my mouth at the time. It started as a joke, but I then began to enjoy the accolades that I was getting, so decided to continue. I am deeply sorry for being such a fraud, and I hope that you will forgive me in time.

Lots of love

Uncle Tom

Needless to say we were all shocked. We felt hugely disappointed, let down, but, most of all, mightily impressed by his deception.

Today was *Cherry Pit Spitting Day,* and a chance for me to use the 'skills' that I learned from my uncle. It was raining, but I bought some cherries and challenged the kids to a cherry pit spitting contest in our back garden. It was not quite as glamorous a location as the camp fire by the pond in northern California, but we had to make do. The kids made their paltry attempts first. Kitty (nearly two) and Layla (six) both managed little more than dribbling their cherry pits on the floor. Leo (three) took a run-up when it was his turn, inhaled by mistake, and we had to slap him on the back to prevent him from choking. Rachel's gallant effort hit the base of the rotary washing line in the middle of the lawn, and then it was my turn. They all watched in awe as my cherry pit soared through the air and into the bushes at the back of the garden.

'Woah,' said Leo.

'That was awesome!' said Layla.

'Awesome,' repeated Kitty.

'How did you... ?' said Rachel, before a glimmer of recognition filled her face. 'Oh yes, your uncle taught you that, didn't he?'

'He sure did. I learned from the best. Hey, kids, watch this,' I said, as I changed direction this time, and 'spat' my pit over our garden wall, over our neighbours Doug and Chris's garden, and onto the roof of the shed in the garden three doors up.

'Wow, Daddy, you are amazing! How DID you do that?' asked Layla.

'Yes, how DID you do that?' said Rachel with her arms folded and her eyebrows raised.

'Well, you have to roll up your tongue tightly, and then blow the pit through your tongue in a short, sharp blow so that it acts like a peashooter. Like this,' I said, and sent one up onto the roof of our house.

'You are so good at that,' said Leo. 'I wish I could spit them as far as you. You are Super Dad.'

'Super Dad,' said Kitty.

A lot of blowing, slobbering, shouting and crying followed, whilst the children attempted to master my technique.

Rachel continued to glare at me. I did feel slightly guilty, and considered owning up straightaway, but I too was revelling in the glory far too much. I'll continue to be Super Dad for a little while longer.

July 7th

'Have you seen what day it is today?' asked Rachel in the kitchen.

'*Chocolate Day*?' I said.

'Not just that. It's *Tell the Truth Day*.'

'Is it?'

'Yes. I think it's time you came clean about your cherry pit spitting powers.'

'Really? Already? They will be so disappointed in me.'

'It's only fair. Leo has been out there already this morning practising. If you don't tell them then I will celebrate this holiday for you.'

'Ok, I'll tell them.'

I broke the news about my deceit to Layla, Leo and Kitty and they were all a bit annoyed that I had cheated, but equally excited that they too had now discovered a sneaky new trick.

My status as a role-model was seriously diminished in the eyes of my children, though, and I was no longer Super Dad. I needed to find a way to regain their admiration. It was time for me to bring out my prized newspaper cutting. I had been saving this until they were a little bit older, but desperate times called for desperate measures.

The proudest moment of my football career - probably my life - came when our local newspaper ran a full page article on the week's local football results, under the headline *MAHOOD ON FIRE AS STANLEY SHATTER REAL*. My team - Abington Stanley FC - had recorded our biggest ever victory against a struggling bunch of no-hopers called Real Roochers Reserves, and I had scored a hat-trick.

I had reached my footballing wonderland. If you ignore the reality that this was a local paper desperate for stories, and forget that we were second from bottom of Division EIGHT of the Northampton Sunday Combination league (there was no

14

Division 9), and overlook the truth that the 'Real' it refers to is not Real Madrid but Real Roochers Reserves who regularly conceded 10 goals or more, then it was a pretty special moment.

I fondly remember, as a child, a newspaper cutting that my dad had kept of him winning a snooker tournament. There was a picture of him standing proudly with a trophy by a snooker table. I used to think of him as being a professional snooker player alongside the likes of Steve Davis and Jimmy White, and assumed this was a prestigious national tournament that he had won. His picture was in the PAPER after all. It wasn't until many years later that I realised it was a snooker tournament for the staff of the department of the hospital in which he worked; but by that time it didn't matter, as he was already a hero to me.

'Wow!' said Leo, as I proudly read out my newspaper cutting to them.

'I knew you played football, Daddy, but I didn't realise you were THAT good,' said Layla.

'Well, I don't like to boast about it,' I said.

'This is so cool. I can't believe you were in the paper. I'm going to tell all my friends,' said Layla.

'You really are Super Dad,' said Leo.

'Super Dad,' shouted Kitty.

'Well done, Super Dad,' said Rachel, resting a hand on my shoulder. 'Are you happy now?'

'Very,' I said.

July 8th

We accepted an offer on our house today. It was exciting to think that we had almost sold our house, but also a little scary that we didn't actually have a house to move to. We had both agreed that we were going to move down to Devon and find somewhere to rent. The problem is that there are very few affordable, long-term rental properties on the market. Because the area is a popular holiday destination, houses often get let out at inflated prices during the summer months, rather than year-round lets. We wanted to find somewhere before the end of August, so that we could be down there in time for the start of Layla's school year, and Leo starting pre-school. We were fairly optimistic that we would find something in time.

July 10th

It was *Don't Step On a Bee Day* - possibly the most meaningless holiday of the year. Not that I think we shouldn't step on bees, but it's surely one of those instinctive things that people do every day of the year. The thing about bees is that not only do they sting, but they also FLY. Most of their time is spent in the air, so it is fairly difficult to step on a bee, even if you wanted to.

Later in the afternoon, I walked to pick up our eldest daughter Layla from school. Treading carefully, I managed to get the whole way there and back without stepping on a single bee.

As Layla rushed towards me, she proudly thrust a piece of paper in my face, on which was a drawing. It was a picture of a car, and surrounding the car were assorted objects. Underneath the drawing she had written the caption: *'Daddy throwing junk out of the car.'*

'What on earth is this?' I asked as we walked through the playground.

'It's a picture. Do you like it?'

'Yes, I know it's a picture. But why does it say that I'm throwing junk out of the car?'

'Because that's what you do,' she said, nonchalantly.

'No I don't. When have you seen me throwing junk out of the car?'

'All the time,' she said, and I realised that some of the mums that we were walking alongside were listening in on our conversation and looking at me disapprovingly.

'I have never thrown junk out of the car. Ever. Why would you say that?' I said, extra loudly so that the onlookers would hear.

'Yes you do. I watch you from the window.'

'Why are you saying that? I don't do that.'

'You do! I watched you do it the other day.'

'Where did you watch me from?'

'The window.'

'The car window? When?'

'No, not the car window. The house window.'

'You watched me from the house window? How?'

'That's what our teacher told us to draw. What we can see when we look out of the window.'

'Do you mean you've watched me from the sitting room window when I'm clearing out all of the rubbish from our car parked outside?'

'Yes, that's what I said. Daddy throwing junk out the car.'

'Yes, darling, but this picture implies that I throw it out of the car window when it's moving along.'

'No, you don't do that. That would be naughty.'

'I know it would. Did your teacher not say anything?'

'Yes, she said that people should never throw junk out of the car.'

'And what did you tell her?'

'I told her you do it all the time.'

We walked straight back to Layla's classroom and had a quiet word with the teacher to explain that I wasn't a fly-tipper. I'm not sure that she believed me.

To take advantage of the sunny weather, we had our dinner outside. As I was helping to clear the plates away, I noticed a bee staggering around the patio table. There was no danger of me stepping on it, but it didn't look very healthy. I had read recently that when bees look in a bad way, they are often just dehydrated, and a drop of sugary water can help revive them.

Sure enough, the bee appeared to slurp at the teaspoon that I rested in front of it, and minutes later, it took to the air. Not only had I avoided stepping on any bees, I had saved a bee's life.

July 11th

I was contacted by a film producer last month about turning my first book - Free Country - into a feature film. After the initial excitement, there had been a few issues raised with the contract. These had all been ironed out, but I was still a bit unsure about the whole thing. Negotiations had been left up in the air while he was abroad working on another production.

I received an email from him today asking if I had made a decision. I had hoped that I would have decided by now, but I was still in two minds. I contacted a couple of people to ask for advice, and was still waiting to hear back from them, so I sent the producer a polite email asking if he could give me another 48 hours.

He replied and insisted that he needed to know immediately - which was a little strange considering he had previously told me he was stacked up with work until after September.

It was *Simplicity Day*. The day honours American author and philosopher Henry David Thoreau, who is most famous for his book *Walden,* in which he reflects on the idea of simple living. Rather than actually reading his book, I took Thoreau's advice and simplified things by reading about his work on Wikipedia instead.

To celebrate this holiday, I did what Thoreau would have done. It was a tenuous link, but I felt that the pressure being put on me to make a decision was adding complications to an already busy month. I made the tough decision to turn the film producer down. Perhaps I was waving goodbye to the only chance of my book being made into a film, but I wasn't prepared to be pushed into making a decision I would later regret.

I reluctantly clicked *'send',* and a few minutes later had quite a bitter reply saying I had been wasting his time, and I should have told him this before he had the contract drawn up. I resisted pointing out that I hadn't had any issues or concerns about his motives until after the contract was drawn up.

Oh well, Free Country - The Movie might make it onto the big screen one day, but unfortunately not just yet. But for now, my life was simplified and I felt remarkably happier about it.

July 13th

I photographed my first female civil partnership today. I had been excited by the prospect for a while, but I had not anticipated how much fun it would be.

It was a day of two halves. The ceremony was extremely intimate, with only 12 immediate family members present. They then sat down for a meal together, before the celebrations took a more exciting turn with the arrival of 100 guests at 4pm. The guests included TWO women's rugby teams, for which one of the couple played for, and resulted in a spontaneous game of rugby amongst the guests, including the happy couple. Not enough weddings have impromptu rugby matches, in my opinion. It should become a traditional ritual of the day. Perhaps just after the cutting of the cake.

The first dance was interrupted by a 7ft drag queen, who performed a surprise 20 minute singing set, and then one of the couple grabbed a microphone and serenaded the other on the dance floor. Every other wedding that I photograph in future will be dull in comparison.

Bald men at weddings are often quite self-conscious when I take their photograph. They frequently make a comment such as 'is the sun reflecting off my head?' or 'can you Photoshop some hair onto me please?' I usually do an awkward laugh, and then make some comment that they look great, without trying to draw further attention to their lack of hair.

Today was *Bald Is In Day* so I tried a new technique.

Sure enough, there were plenty of men lacking in the hair department, and after being caught taking a candid photo of one of them, he turned to me and said:

'Oi! I hope you can do something to the picture to bring back my hair.'

Rather than my usual uncomfortable response, I simply looked at him, pointed a finger in his direction and said:

'Hey man, bald is IN.'

'You are so right!' he said with a smile, as I walked off like a Wild West gunslinger.

'See, I told you bald was in,' I heard him say to his wife as I moved on to find my next bald victim.

It is going to be my new response from now on.

July 14th

'George! Quick! Come here!' said Rachel, slightly panicked at the front door.

I looked down the stairs to see a man sitting on our doorstep with his back to the door, hunched over, with his head on his knees.

'Who is he?' I asked, making my way towards him.

'No idea. I just opened the front door and he was sitting there.'

'Hi mate. Are you ok?' I called.

There was no answer. I moved towards him and put a hand on his shoulder.

No response.

I gave him a gentle shake and the movement caused his body to slump forward even further. Shit. Was he dead? I shook him slightly more vigorously this time and asked him again if he was ok. His head lifted slightly and he slurred something at me and then went back to sleep.

'Do you think we should call an ambulance?' asked Rachel.

'I don't think so. I think he's just very, very drunk.'

'But he's wearing shorts and trainers. Are you sure he hasn't been out for a run and collapsed.'

'If he went out for a run, then it was several days ago and he got somewhat sidetracked. He stinks and there's a can of beer and a cigarette next to him.'

I took a quick photo - it would have been rude not to - before trying again to wake him.

'Come on, buddy, let's get you up. Do you know where you live?' I asked.

The couple whose offer we had accepted were coming to have another look at the house shortly, and I didn't want the sale to fall through because of a resident drunk on the doorstep.

He looked at me. His eyes barely open.

'Yes. Yes,' he muttered, and then garbled something in a language I didn't understand.

'Would you like some WATER? Is there anyone I can PHONE for you?' I said, as I tried to help him to his feet.

'No. S'ok,' he said and then staggered off down the street, bouncing off walls and parked cars as he went.

I watched him for a few minutes to make sure he didn't stumble into the road. He tried to use his keys to get into another house a few doors down, and eventually realised that it wasn't his house either, so sat down on the new doorstep and went to sleep.

It was *National Nude Day*. Thankfully he wasn't observing it.

I walked around the house naked for the rest of the morning, much to Rachel's annoyance.

'I thought we were all going to the park?' asked Rachel.

'Yes, we are,' I said.

'And are you going to go like that?'

'I might.'

'Bet you wouldn't dare.'

My eyes lit up at the prospect of proving her wrong and winning the bet.

'No, you're right,' I conceded.

'Remember that the couple are coming to look at our house again this morning?'

'I know, I know. I obviously won't answer the door like this.'

'Err... you do remember that the estate agent still has his own key, don't you?'

I heard footsteps on the street and put my clothes on quicker than I ever have before.

July 15th

St. Swithin was a Saxon Bishop of Winchester. Legend has it that he asked to be buried outside because he wanted to be rained and trodden on. His wish was granted, but nine years later, the monks decided to build an ornate shrine inside the cathedral, and attempted to relocate his remains there on 15th

July, 971. It is claimed that there was a heavy rainstorm on this day.

It became folklore that if it rained on *St. Swithin's Day* it will continue to rain for another 40 days, but if it stays dry, 40 days of good weather will follow.

'St. Swithin's day if thou dost rain
For forty days it will remain
St. Swithin's day if thou be fair
For forty days 'twill rain nae mair.'

Today was *St. Swithin's Day* and it stayed dry all day, which means we are in for a glorious summer.

I filled in the forms for the solicitors to commence the conveyancing for our house and then faxed them over. Yes, I know, check me out, I'm so state-of-the-art with my fax machine.

The solicitors called to say that they needed me to post, or hand-deliver, the original copy of our marriage certificate in order for it to be certified. Our marriage certificate is one of a few things in our house that gets filed away correctly. Ever since an incident with it after our honeymoon I have looked after it very carefully.

We got back from our honeymoon and Rachel needed our marriage certificate in order to change the details on her passport, driving licence and bank. We searched the entire house but could not locate it anywhere.

In a last ditch attempt, simply because there was nowhere else to look, I brought in the bins from outside, having just put them out for the following day's collection. There, squashed between an empty box of Weetabix and some takeaway menus in the paper recycling box, was our marriage certificate. We had only been back at our house for less than an hour the day after our wedding, before heading off on our honeymoon, and in that time, Rachel had managed to 'file' our marriage certificate in the recycling bin. It has become a recurring theme since. She put my very first Amazon royalty cheque in the bin, a mortgage application, and my tax-return.

'It's because you always leave bits of paper lying around. If they stay on the table long enough then they go in the recycling bin. Those are the rules,' she said.

'But I gave the marriage certificate to you. You were looking after it.'

'Yes, well all of the other incidents were your own fault.'

'What about the £50 of Abington Stanley Football Club subs that I brought back from football.'

'Bits of paper. Left lying around. Like I just said.'

'But that was £50 worth of £1 coins.'

'Yes, but they were in an envelope.'

To avoid further incidents like this, important paper documents now have a special place in the filing cabinet where Rachel won't have the temptation to dispose of them.

This afternoon, I climbed onto my bike - the trusty Falcon - as my other bike had a flat tyre, and cycled the two miles across town in the blazing heat to the solicitor's office to drop off the marriage certificate. A young work-experience lad met me at the door, thanked me, and took the envelope from me.

I then cycled back across town, stopping on three occasions to readjust The Falcon's handlebars that kept slipping to one side. At the exact second that I reached my front door, my mobile phone started ringing in my pocket.

'Hello,' I said. I did answer my phone first, by the way.

'Hi. It's Chris. I'm just ringing to confirm that we have received a copy of your marriage certificate in the post and we have taken a certified copy. When would you like to collect it?'

'Sorry, what do you mean you received it in the post? I hand-delivered it to you a few minutes ago. Have you finished with it already?'

'Yes, that's correct. When would you like to collect it?'

'Err, now I guess. I'll be with you in ten minutes,' I said.

The incompetence of our solicitor didn't bode well for the successful completion of the house sale.

July 17th

July 17th is our wedding anniversary and I was fairly certain Rachel had forgotten all about it. She has a habit of forgetting our anniversary, which pleases me immensely, as it gives me ammunition to use against her when required. On the years that she has remembered, it was usually because someone has reminded her the day before, leaving her no time to get me a card or present.

There had been no mention of our anniversary in recent weeks, but her sister called over to visit yesterday, so I assumed it would have come up in conversation, as, unlike Rachel, her sister manages to remember all important dates. Rachel was either playing the same game as me, or, yet again, had no idea.

Last night she went out for a drink with a friend. While she was gone, Rachel's parents kindly brought round an anniversary present.

In the morning, I got up with the kids at 6:30am, and left Rachel to have a bit of a lie in. At 7:30am she came downstairs, and as she entered the living room I greeted her with 'Happy Anniversary!' and gave her a big cuddle and kiss; a look of bewilderment crossed her face.

'Is it today? What date is it?'

'July 17th. I knew you'd forgotten.'

'Is it really today? I'm so sorry. Why didn't anyone remind me?'

'That's alright. Your parents remembered. They dropped around a present last night. And here's a card from your sister.'

'Oh god. How embarrassing. I'm so, so sorry.'

'That's ok. Here's a little something for you,' I said, handing her a present.

'That's very sweet of you. Thank you,' she said, giving me a hug. 'I'm so mortified. Happy anniversary! Weirdly I was talking about wedding anniversaries in the pub last night.'

'And it still didn't click?'

'No. I'm rubbish, I know. I can't believe it's been eight years.'

'Nine,' I said. 'Nine years.'

'Really? I thought we got married in 2005?'

'2004.'

'Oops. Oh dear.'

This was one of the reasons I fell in love with Rachel. Anniversaries are nice, but they are fairly meaningless and superficial. Rachel can be a little scatty, but that is part of her charm. She doesn't care too much about the trivial things in life.

A work colleague once asked her what type of car she had. Rachel had driven the same car for four years but was completely stumped by the question. She thought long and hard about it and eventually responded 'a red one.'

We had been keeping a close eye on property websites, hoping to find a house to rent, but there had been nothing available. Today we received notification of a place that looked ideal. There was only one photo of it, but the specification sounded more than adequate. We lived 250 miles away, so viewing properties was going to be a challenge. It just so happened that my parents were on holiday in Devon for the week, so I phoned them to see if there was any chance that they could view the house for us.

July 18th

It was 13:45pm and Rachel was at work. I was in the process of getting the two younger children ready to go to Layla's school for 2pm to watch her Sports Day. My phone rang. It was my mum.

'Hi Dordie Wardie,' she said (Dordie Wardie is what my family call me after I pronounced my name Dord when I was a baby. Over the years it became Dordie Wardie, and my family still call me it. I'm 34.)

'Hi Mum.'

'Can you talk?'

'Err... yes. We're just getting ready to go to Sports Day.'

'Ok, I'll be quick. We went to look at The Vicarage and it's absolutely perfect.'

'Really? Tell me more,' I said, as I tried to put Kitty's pants, on whilst balancing the phone on my shoulder. I was putting the pants on HER, alright. Not me, you weirdo.

'It's got four bedrooms, a big garden with a rope swing. Nice kitchen. A garage. It is seriously perfect. Dad thought so too. Even if you were only renting it, I can see it's the kind of place you could happily live in for years.'

'It sounds great. We'll have to try and arrange to come and look at it.'

'That's the problem. They've got another viewing at 2pm today.'

'But that's in 10 minutes.'

'I know. I think you should go for it. Trust us, you'd love it. Did I mention it had a rope swing?'

28

'Yes you did. Oh, I don't know. I can't make a decision like that. Rachel's at work and I won't be able to get hold of her, and I'm just off out the door. What would we have to do if we wanted it?'

'I would ring the estate agent and they would forward you an application to fill in. They want the place filled quickly, so the sooner you can make a decision the better.'

'Ok then. Let's go for it. I'm sure Rachel won't mind. Thanks.'

'Great. I'll ring them for you now.'

Layla's Sports Day was fun, but hard work with two children who didn't want to sit still and watch their big sister doing the egg and spoon race, crawl through hoops, throw beanbags into a bucket and run around cones. I also couldn't stop thinking about the house. Who decides to rent a house having not even viewed it, seen any internal photos, or discussed it with their wife? It was a bit of a rash decision but I didn't have much choice.

Once we were back home, I distracted the children with the TV and snacks, whilst I frantically tried to fill in the application form - providing evidence of income, credit history, employment details and references. I cleverly phoned my best friend's dad who is a vicar, to ask if he would provide a reference for us if required. The Vicarage is still owned by the diocese, so having a vicar as a referee would do us no harm.

Rachel returned home from work at 4:30pm.

'Hello. How was your day? What are you up to?' she asked.

'Hi. My day was ok thanks. I'm renting us a house. I hope that's ok. I didn't have time to run it past you. I'm just trying to get these application forms off ASAP.'

'A house? What do you mean?'

'You know that old Vicarage? Mum and Dad went to look at it, and said it was perfect.'

'Really? I loved the sound of that one. Shouldn't we go and look at it first?'

'There's no time. Someone else has already looked at it this afternoon, so it's now or never. Did you know it has a rope swing?'

'Ok. Let's go for it. I'm excited. I had a good feeling about that place.'

'Me too. Don't get your hopes up just yet, though. The other people might want it too, and then it'll be up to the landlords to decide.'

I submitted all the relevant forms by 4:45pm and we took the kids to McDonald's to celebrate Rachel's last day at the school in which she has taught for eight years (yes we go to McDonald's as a celebration. Don't judge us). She was understandably quite emotional about the whole thing (leaving the school, not McDonald's), as she had become very close to all of the teachers and pupils.

Nelson Mandela Day was created in 2009 on July 18th (his birthday) in honour of the great man and what he achieved. It is not just a day to admire the legacy that Mandela created, but to celebrate the notion that every individual - whatever their background - has the ability to change the world.

To celebrate *Nelson Mandela Day*, I tried explaining apartheid to Layla and Leo, but they didn't really understand. One of the many benefits of living in urban Britain is the huge ethnic diversity. There are over 25 languages spoken at Layla's primary school, and the concept of racial segregation is thankfully completely incomprehensible to her.

July 19th

'I couldn't sleep last night,' said Rachel. 'I was so excited about that house. I'll be gutted if we don't get it.'

'Me too. What if the landlord doesn't like the sound of us?' I said.

'Why wouldn't they?'

'They might want someone a bit more, you know, professional.'

'What did you put down on the form about our occupations?'

'I wrote photographer/author for me, and primary school teacher for you.'

'See, what's wrong with that? I'm glad you mentioned author. I bet they'll love the idea of having someone 'creative' living there.'

'Really? I think if I was a landlord and someone wrote photographer and author, I would think they sounded like a dick. I would much prefer a doctor, lawyer, accountant or office worker, or anyone with a 'real' job.'

'Maybe you're right.'

'And although you are a primary school teacher, aren't you technically unemployed now?'

'Not until September.'

'Either way, we probably don't sound like the most reliable of candidates.'

Rachel took the kids to visit her mum whilst I tried to work, but in reality I spent the morning pressing F5 on my computer to check for new emails, even though it refreshes itself every minute automatically.

I was just about to go and make some lunch when an email arrived from the estate agents. An intense feeling of nervousness raced through my body. It's a feeling that I haven't experienced since collecting exam results at school. I was too anxious to open it. Should I wait until Rachel got home? I took a quick walk around the house before realising that no amount of delaying or diversion tactics could actually change what was written in the email, so I clicked it straight open.

Dear George,

Thank you for sending through the application. We have discussed it with the Landlord, and unfortunately they have decided to go with another applicant.

We would like to wish you the best of luck in finding another property.

Kind Regards,

Matthew

My heart sank. Why? What was wrong with us? Who were the other applicants and what made them special? I should not have written 'author' on the form. How pretentious of me. Who would want a bloody author as a tenant? What a complete and utter dick I was.

After writing my letter of complaint to the Archdeacon back in January about one of his vicars, I couldn't help thinking that this was the church's karma coming back to bite me on the ass.

For the first time, we both had a slight sense of apprehension that the move to Devon might not be as simple as we had hoped.

July 20th

'OH MY GOD!' shouted Rachel. 'Quickly, come down here.'

'What is it?' I called from upstairs, as I tried to get ready to photograph a wedding.

'Come here!'

'Not another drunk on the doorstep, is it?'

I hurried downstairs and found Rachel and the three children all with their noses squashed against the patio doors.

'It's a rat, Daddy,' said Layla.

'A rat? Really, where?'

'Just there,' said Rachel, pointing to the rat, which was just there.

A fairly big, slightly scraggy-looking rat was strolling casually around the patio that stretches down the side of our kitchen. Now I know you are supposed to be *'never more than six feet from a rat'*, or whatever that statistic is, but we don't tend to get them in our garden very often. In fact, having lived in Northampton almost all of my life, I don't think I have ever seen a rat 'in the wild'.

Engineers had been doing major excavation work on the sewers outside our house for past few weeks. It involved digging a giant access tunnel, and then blasting air into a giant plastic sleeve that lines the sewer walls. Needless to say, the rats were fairly incensed with having their home lined with wall-to-wall plastic, especially when it was being applied by a machine as loud as a jet engine. They decided to seek accommodation elsewhere. The lady across the street from us mentioned that a rat had got into her house, and now one had taken a fancy to our patio.

'What are we going to do with it, Daddy?' asked Leo.

'I'm not sure. But I think it needs to go back to where it came from.'

'We could try and catch it in a bucket?' suggested Rachel.

'How would we do that?' I asked.

'We could corner it and then scoop it up in the bucket.'

'And then what would we do with it?'

'I don't know. Take it to the park and let it out there?'

'Take it to the park?' I laughed. 'I'd love to see you walking to the park with a rat in a bucket. That's the best thing I've heard in ages.'

'Why?' asked Rachel, slightly offended.

'Don't you think it would escape?'

'From a bucket? How? It's got slippery sides.'

'Go on then. You have a go at catching it in a bucket. I'll watch.'

'How did it get in our garden?' asked Layla.

'Good question,' I said. 'It must have found a way out of a drain somehow, I guess.'

'We could call the council. I'm sure they sort out rat problems. They are a health hazard, aren't they?'

'Maybe, but I think they just deal with infestations, rather than just coming round for a lone rat. Where has it gone now?'

'There!' said Kitty, who was completely transfixed. 'Under Leo's bike.'

'I don't want the rat on my bike. Get off, you silly rat,' shouted Leo, banging on the glass.

'I've got an idea. We'll lift the manhole cover and usher it back down into the sewer,' I said.

'How do you usher a rat?' asked Rachel.

'I haven't worked that bit out yet.'

I used a screwdriver to prise the lid off the manhole and slid it to one side, exposing the network of channels that led to the sewers.

'Right, kids, you all stay inside. Rachel, you stand guard by the manhole. You can use this spade to stop it getting past you.

34

I'm going to get it to run towards you and hopefully it will go down the hole.'

'What if it runs at me?' said Rachel.

'Use the spade!'

'I'm not going to hit it.'

'You don't have to hit it. You can just use it to stop it running up your legs.'

'Oh god. If it runs up my legs then I'm definitely going to hit it.'

By this point, the rat had found its way into the recycling box, and was having a good rummage around. I poked the box with a stick and it leaped out of the box, ran straight across my bare toes, and then towards the manhole. Rachel shrieked, which caused the rat to skid to a halt, before it darted back towards me, taking refuge near a drain cover below our kitchen window. I banged the drainpipe with a broom, but there was no sign of it. There was only one possible explanation; it had gone up one of the pipes.

'Where do all of those pipes come from?' asked Rachel, the three children all still standing fascinated at the patio door.

'One is the main drainpipe from the roof. Another is from the kitchen sink, and that one is from the washing machine.'

'You mean that the rat might have got into our washing machine? Or even our sink? That's revolting.'

'I think the washing machine and sink pipes are too narrow, hopefully. It must have gone up the drainpipe. I'll run the bathroom tap and see if I can flush it out.'

The drainpipe went up the wall of the house, as most drainpipes do, and at the halfway point it was fed by the overflow midway junction box (I just made that name up), where the pipes from the sink and the bath also fed into it. I ran both the sink tap and the bath tap, and peered out of the window to watch as the water poured down through the overflow midway junction box and into the drainpipe.

'Any sign of it?' I shouted down to Rachel.

'No, nothing. Where could it have gone?'

I turned off the taps and then waited a few minutes.

After a while I saw something move at the top of the drainpipe. Slowly but surely, the rat heaved its soggy body out of the pipe, and sat in the corner of the overflow midway junction box wiping itself with its paws (or whatever rats feet are called. Feet probably) and looking extremely sorry for itself.

'It's out! It's made it all the way up the drainpipe. Poor thing, it's absolutely drenched.'

'How did it climb up there when all the water was going down it?' asked Rachel.

'It's pretty determined. And you thought you would be able to keep it in a bucket.'

'Ok. Perhaps the bucket was a bad idea.'

'Can I see it, Daddy? Pleeeeasse,' said Layla.

'Pleeeeease,' said Leo.

'Pleeeeease,' repeated Kitty.

'Ok then. Come upstairs.'

One by one I lifted them up to the bathroom window so they could take a look at Mr Ratty.

'Oh, it's so cute,' said Layla. 'Can we keep it as a pet?'

'No. We can't keep it as a pet. It's a rat.'

'But Charlie at school has got a rat.'

'Yes, but that will be a pet rat from a pet shop. Not a rat from a sewer.'

'Ohhhh. But look it's so cute.'

She was right. It was actually quite cute, in a weird rodenty sort of way. Not cute enough for me to want it to hang around, though.

I got a bamboo cane from the shed, leaned out of the window, and carefully gave the rat a gentle prod. It disappeared down the drainpipe in a split second, and re-emerged at the bottom before taking refuge behind the barbecue.

I went downstairs and tried again unsuccessfully to encourage it down the manhole. Instead, it found its way back up the drainpipe, before reappearing in the overflow midway junction box seconds later. It had disappeared up the drainpipe as quick as, well, a rat up a drainpipe.

'Perhaps we should try ringing the council,' Rachel suggested again. 'Shouldn't you have left for your wedding by now?'

'Yes, but I don't want to leave you all with this rat about. We could call the council, but they won't come and catch it and re-home it. They will just put down rat poison and kill it.'

'No! We can't kill Mr Ratty. He is so sweet. Please don't kill him,' said Layla.

'No! We LOVE Mr Ratty,' said Leo.

'We wuv Mr Watty,' said Kitty.

We didn't want it killed, but it couldn't stay either. I had time for one last try before I really was going to be late for the wedding. I don't think the couple would have seen rat-catching as an acceptable excuse for missing their big day.

For my final attempt, I used two plastic lids from the sandpit propped up with bricks, and positioned at an angle between the walls and the open manhole. There was no way for Mr Ratty to get past, other than contending with the open manhole (incidentally, *'manhole'* is a really weird word when you think about it. Actually, try not to think about it too much).

Anyway, I went back up to the bathroom window, gave him a prod with my cane, and he scurried back down the drainpipe. I watched from above as he emerged slowly and headed back towards the barbecue. I was about to go downstairs to block the drainpipe, when he started sniffing along the wall between our house and Doug's, before reaching my strategically placed bricks. He worked his way along the sandpit lid, reached the open manhole, peered inside, had a little sniff of the air, and jumped down.

Rachel and the kids cheered and whooped from behind the patio door, and I did a Tim Henman style fist pump on my own in the bathroom. I then went downstairs and we had a group hug.

'Mr Ratty has gone back to his family, hasn't he Daddy?' said Leo.

'He sure has. He'll be a very happy Mr Ratty. Well that was fun, wasn't it? Right, I'd better go before I'm too late.'

'Err, hadn't you better shut the manhole cover first?' said Rachel. 'Otherwise Mr Ratty AND his family might all be waiting for you when you get home.'

'Ah, yes. Good point.'

I have just written 1700 words about a rat. I would like to redeem it all by claiming that coincidently it was *National Rat Day*, or *World Rodent Appreciation Month*, but the truth is it was neither of those. It was *National Lollipop Day* and *National Hotdog Day*, and this rat had no connection whatsoever to either of these. Sometimes, however, the most random and tedious of tasks can turn into the highlight of the day. And no amount of lollipops or hot dogs was going to trump the feeling of reuniting Mr Ratty with his family.

I did of course have a hotdog and lollipop for dinner.

July 21st

There is an urban legend that McDonald's sells a burger not listed on any of their menus. Yet it still exists and can be ordered at any of its outlets.

The McGangBang.

I had heard rumours about the McGangBang many times over the years, but I had never tasted one. The elusive burger was said to consist of a Mayo Chicken burger INSIDE a Double Cheeseburger. You put the entire Mayo Chicken - bun and all - in between the two burgers of the Double Cheeseburger.

I had to have one.

It was *National Junk Food Day* and it didn't take much persuasion for the family to take a trip to the Golden Arches for a traditional Sunday lunch.

It is claimed that staff at McDonald's know all about the McGangBang and will happily assemble one for you when ordered. I queued up at the counter, more nervous than I thought possible at a fast food counter, and then it was time to place my order.

'Hello. What can I get you today?' asked the smiley young lady. I couldn't decide whether I would prefer to be asking a male or female employee for a McGangBang. I didn't have a choice now.

'Hello. Could I have three Fish-Finger Happy Meals please - all with orange juice. A Quarter Pounder with Cheese Meal with a Coke, and then a... er... er... a Mc...' I paused, looking either side of me before I spoke. There were two young children with their mum to one side, and an elderly couple on the other.

'... and a Mayo Chicken and a Double Cheeseburger... and another Coke,' I said, wimping out and ordering them separately.

'Mayo Chicken and a Double Cheeseburger, was that?' she asked, raising her eyebrows with a very slight smirk that suggested *'I know your game. I know what you've got planned.'*

'Yes, thank you. That's everything.'

She handed me the tray with a smile and said 'Enjoy your meal'.

'I'm sure I will,' I said.

At our table I built my behemoth. It looked immense. I bit into the beast, which was an endeavour in itself; it was well worth the effort. It was a strange sensation and a bizarre combination of textures, but it definitely worked. The McGangBang was a triumph, *Junk Food Day* was a guilty success, and I hoped that I would be able to order a McGangBang by name one day.

July 22nd

Bizarrely, July 22nd is *Ratcatcher's Day*. If I had known, I would have left Mr Ratty where he was for a couple more days, and tried to catch him on the designated day instead.

Ratcatcher's Day is celebrated either on June 26th, or July 22nd, to commemorate the myth of the Pied Piper of Hamelin. The difference in dates is due to the Brothers Grimm using the June date in their tale, and Robert Browning using the July date in his version.

It then dawned on me that it didn't matter that our rat incident had occurred two days previously. It wasn't *Catch A Rat Day*, it was *Ratcatcher's Day*. I was a rat catcher, so it was therefore MY day.

'It's *Ratcatcher's Day* today,' I said to Rachel.

'Ha, that's strange. Well you obviously celebrated that one a few days early.'

'Not necessarily. I'm still a rat catcher, and this is a day for rat catchers. So, it's basically MY special day.'

'But you didn't catch a rat.'

'What do you mean?'

'I mean, we had a rat, and you successfully got rid of it, but you didn't technically catch it.'

'You're just nitpicking. I'm still a rat catcher. I can do what I want today.'

'Like what?'

'I don't know. I might just spend the day on the sofa.'

'But you agreed to take Leo and Kitty swimming.'

'Well, that was before I realised it was *Ratcatcher's Day*.'

'You didn't catch a rat! If you can catch a rat with your bare hands, then you can do whatever you like today. If not, then you can take the kids swimming like you promised. I've got some chores to do around the house.'

'But this day commemorates the Pied Piper of Hamelin, and he didn't technically catch rats either. He just got rid of them, just like I did,' I said, with a smug grin, thinking I'd won the argument.

'Fair enough. Well, if you can get a load of rats to follow you whilst you play a musical instrument, then it can be your special day,' said Rachel, with a look that showed she had unequivocally won.

'Leo? Kitty? Let's go swimming.'

41

July 23rd

The Duke and Duchess of Cambridge gave birth to a baby boy today. I am not a royalist, and I admit that the royal family serve little purpose, but I do still think they are pretty awesome. They are part of what makes this country great.

William and Kate seem like a genuinely cool and down-to-earth couple. I think it would be hard for anyone to hate them.

I hated William with a passion today, though. I watched the live TV coverage of them emerging from the hospital with their brand new baby. With the world's press looking on, William calmly and effortlessly slotted the baby car seat into the back of his Range Rover before driving off. I hated him because installing car seats for the first time is a fucking NIGHTMARE, and he made it look easy.

The first time I fitted ours it took me almost an entire morning to decipher the complex set of 34 badly-drawn illustrations in the Chinese instruction manual. It drove me absolutely crazy.

It is possible that William spent many hours behind closed doors, privately weeping, as he couldn't get the seatbelt through slot A, and then slot B without it folding over, but somehow I doubt it.

I do think he would have got a lot more respect from members of the public if he had emerged from the hospital, and then spent several hours fiddling with buckles, seatbelts and a Chinese instruction manual, whilst Kate stood alongside telling him to 'hurry up' every few seconds, before both of them having a complete meltdown and collapsing on the road in a sobbing heap of royalness. People would have warmed to them so much more. Call yourself a man of the people, William? What a shame. You're not like the rest of us.

The country was experiencing its highest temperatures in seven years. Today was *Hot Enough For Ya Day*; a day when you are encouraged - for no apparent reason - to use the phrase 'hot enough for ya'.

The British are notoriously obsessed with the weather, and conversation is often dominated by it. But when the weather is particularly hot, or particularly cold, it is genuinely ALL we talk about.

I am as guilty as everyone else. I make a conscious decision not to mention the weather when I talk to other parents on the school run, or if I bump into our postman Jason in the street, but however hard I try, it is my default topic of conversation.

At least today I had a scripted phrase I could use, so I didn't even have to generate an opinion on the weather.

'Hot enough for ya, Jason?' I said, as I signed for the delivery of yet another coat that Rachel had ordered (who buys new coats in July?).

'Bit too hot,' said Jason. 'Still, at least it's not raining.'

'Hot enough for ya?' I said to the mums at the school gate. They all just looked at me as if I was slightly mental.

'Yeah... errrr.... mmm,' they muttered.

'Hot enough for ya?' I asked Mr Bharat the man who runs the newsagent where I collect Doug's paper.

'Yes sir,' he said, slightly startled.

I started to like my new phrase. It trims down tedious conversations about the weather into one small bite-sized, almost rhetorical question. I'm sticking with it. Towards the end of the year, when temperatures start to nosedive, I can just switch it to 'cold enough for ya?' The phrase transforms any vague weather conversation into a purposed statement. It can be adapted to suit any weather situation: Wet enough for ya? Cloudy enough for ya? Mild enough for ya? Frosty enough for ya? Snowy enough for ya? Windy enough for ya? Is that enough examples for ya?

July 26th

A new rental property popped up on the internet. We had been hoping for a house in, or at least close to, the local town, as we thought it would make it easier to meet new people. This particular one was out in the sticks, but it definitely had a lot going for it.

I had a busy week with various jobs and meetings, and we would not get an opportunity to go and view it until next week, by which point, it would probably already have been taken.

It was *All or Nothing Day*. I interpreted this as maybe a sign that we should just rent it, even without having a viewing.

'Do you think that's a good idea?' asked Rachel, after I suggested it to her.

'It probably is a stupid idea, but we are running out of options. The school term starts in five weeks.'

'Well I'm keen. It looks like a nice house from the pictures. Let's go for it.'

I phoned the estate agent to ask if the house was still available.

'Yes, it is. It only went on the market this morning,' said the lady, somewhat abruptly.

'Great. We would like to rent it, if that's possible,' I said.

'No, that won't be possible. You will have to fill in an application in order to be considered for a viewing. This property is likely to be extremely popular.'

'Oh, right. And this is an application just to be considered for a viewing?'

'Yes, that's correct.'

'Well could you possibly send me the relevant forms to fill in please?'

'Yes I will, but I have to warn you that there will be a strict vetting process before we decide on a list of candidates to view the property.'

'Ok, I understand.'

The forms were emailed over to me and I spent a couple of hours filling them in and trying to make us sound as professional as possible. I decided not to mention being an author this time.

Rachel was a qualified teacher that would be unemployed in a few weeks. I was a self-employed photographer, who was moving 250 miles away from work that I had spent seven years building up. It didn't even sound very convincing in my own head. How on earth would a heartless estate agent take us seriously? Still, it was worth a shot. Finding somewhere to live was proving a lot harder than we had anticipated.

July 27th

In 1999, a Utah-based artist named Tom Forsythe created a series of photographs of nude Barbie dolls in compromising positions amongst kitchen appliances. Barbie's maker Mattel attempted to sue Forsythe for copyright infringement, and a five year court case took place. The court eventually found in favour of Forsythe, and Mattel were ordered to pay him $1.8 million in legal fees and court costs, stating that Mattel's action was 'frivolous' and 'unreasonable'.

In honour of this, the *Free Culture Foundation* formed *Barbie in a Blender Day* as a celebration of free speech and fair use. People are encouraged to follow in Tom Forsythe's footsteps and take their own photos of Barbies in states of distress.

I had a wedding to photograph, but before that, I had a Barbie to blend.

Layla has a large selection of blonde, generic plastic dolls. I figured she probably wouldn't miss one of them, but in order to establish which her least favourite was, I asked if I could borrow one for Kitty to play with. Sisterly love hasn't yet kicked in from the elder sibling, so I knew she would pass on one that she didn't care about.

Our blender struggles with bananas, so I knew it would not cope with a plastic doll. Having watched a lot of the zombie TV series *The Walking Dead* recently, I decided that a meat-cleaver to the head was a more than adequate substitute.

'Is that one of my dolls?' asked Layla when she heard the thwack of the cleaver onto the wooden chopping board.

'Er... no... it's...'

'It IS one of my dolls. You just hid it under a tea towel.'

'I... I... I had to give her an operation.'

'What do you mean? What sort of an operation?'

'Well, you see her head was, kind of... err... I needed to do some brain surgery on her.'

'Why? She doesn't have a brain. She's a plastic doll. What are you talking about?' she asked, pulling away the tea-towel to reveal a Barbie with the top of her skull missing.

'What have you done? Why did you do that?' she shouted. 'Mummy! Daddy has chopped half of one of my doll's head off.'

She burst into tears.

'Really? I'm sure he wouldn't have done it on purpose,' said Rachel, coming into the kitchen and witnessing the carnage on the side.

'Oh, it seems he did do it on purpose,' she said, with a questioning frown.

'It's *Barbie In a Blender Day*,' I said. 'I'm expressing my free speech.'

'Right. Haven't you got a wedding to go and photograph today?'

'Yes. I'll just clear up this mess first.'

'No, leave it. Just go.'

'Is this a good time to remind you about the time you forgot our wedding anniversary?'

'GO!'

Free speech is a vital privilege, and something that cannot be over-valued, but I would certainly advise against decapitating your daughter's dolls with a meat cleaver. I gained absolutely nothing.

After the wedding ceremony, I checked my phone and saw six missed calls from Rachel, which was a little bit concerning. Surely she couldn't still be angry about the Barbie massacre?

I called her back.

'Is everything ok?' I asked. 'I'm really sorry about Barbie.'

'Yes, fine thanks. It's not about Barbie, although I still think you're a dick. The scary estate agent phoned.'

'Oh god, what did she want?'

'I had to have a proper phone interview with her.'

'A phone interview? What do you mean?'

'She gave me a proper grilling. She wanted to know everything about why we were moving, jobs, finances, references, everything.'

'How did it go? Sorry you had to do that. I didn't know she was going to phone today.'

'I think it went quite well. I think I nailed it.'

'Really?'

'Yes, she seemed quite convinced by my answers, but I think it'll be another few days before they make a decision.'

'And this is just to see if we get a viewing?'

'Yes.'

'Wow. That's ridiculous.'

'I know.'

'Well done anyway. It sounds like it went as well as it possibly could have. I think you would have done a much better job on the phone that I would have.'

'I think so too,' she laughed. 'After the Barbie incident I certainly wouldn't pick you as a tenant.'

'I've learned my lesson. It won't happen again.'

July 28th

I play cricket once a year. I'm not completely opposed to it, but it's not one of my favourite sports, and it takes such a bloody long time. I used to get picked to play for our school team, but I would often make up an excuse to get out of playing, such as a member of my extended family had died. They always looked suspicious when my friend Mark and I seemed to have an awful lot of our relatives dying at the same time, but we were confident knowing that it was not something they would ever follow up or ask us to prove.

On the occasions when I didn't manage to think of an adequate excuse in time, we had to play, and I used to dread the entire day. To make matters significantly worse, we played against schools that had a lot of very talented county cricketers in their sides. Our rival school, Sponne, had a young player by the name of Graeme Swann. He had a reputation of being a natural with both the bat and the ball. Often players were highlighted as being potential stars of the future, but this guy was in a league of his own.

Graeme Swann was technically a spin bowler, but he bowled spin faster than any of the pace bowlers on our team.

It was terrifying to face him. The ball came at you from all angles and you wouldn't even consider trying to score any runs off him. I remember surviving an entire over of his and feeling like I had just hit a century, despite not making contact with the ball once.

When the opposition batted, Graeme Swann went on to score a ridiculous 191, in a 20 over match, before being caught out on the boundary by Mark, who was unexpectedly glad that his imaginary aunt hadn't died that weekend after all.

I have been scarred by cricket ever since. And that young upstart Graeme Swann? I have no idea what happened to him.*

Today I was at the Open University in Milton Keynes, which is the venue for my friend Tom's annual cricket match. He hosts the match around the time of his birthday each year, and gathers a group of his friends together to play against a team of equally hopeless cricketers.

In the practise nets beforehand, despite not picking up a cricket ball since last year's game, I was actually bowling pretty well. My deliveries were all relatively straight, and with a decent amount of pace and accuracy. I was feeling pretty confident.

Our team batted first and the opening four batsmen put on a decent number of runs between them. They then introduced a new bowler who bowled our highest run scorer, Mike, out first ball. He then removed our captain, and most experienced batsmen, Tom, with his next ball, before dispatching Gibbo for his hat-trick. One minute I was sitting in the sun thinking that there was little chance I would be required to bat, and the next I was frantically padding up and heading out to the crease gripped with fear.

'Watch out. This guy is bloody good,' said Gibbo as we passed on the outfield.

49

The first ball came at me ridiculously quickly and I prodded it away like a seasoned pro. The second was identical, and again I managed to block it with my bat. The final one I took a swing at and missed, but it fizzed inches over the stumps and I survived the over. Feelings of those school matches against 'Swanny' returned, and I suddenly felt invincible. This bowler had dispatched three decent batsmen in three balls, and I had survived a further three balls unscathed. I knew I could potentially build a respectable innings.

Their next bowler was a young boy, aged about 11, and he looked like he was playing cricket for the very first time. His bowling was horrendous, and I relished the chance to score some runs off him. A couple of big hits from Damo followed at the other end, and then it was my turn to face. The ball pitched up nicely a long way from the stumps and I skipped down the wicket ready to hit it out of the ground. But I took an air-shot, and turned around to watch the ball gently clip the leg stump and the bails toppled to the ground. I had to make the walk of shame back to the pavilion, having scored no runs, and been bowled out by a child.

Thankfully, our remaining batsmen put on a decent show, and we built a respectable target for the opposition to chase.

And then it was our turn to bowl.

Our team's bowlers took a few early wickets, and it started to look like it was going to be a whitewash. Tom suggested that I have a bowl, and, having taken a wicket the previous year, I was happy to have a go.

The first ball flew well wide of the batsman, which was fairly common for a first ball. I was just getting my eye in. Or so I hoped.

The next ball went even wider. The next wider still. I then bowled a ball that flew several feet over the wicket keeper's head, without even bouncing, and almost hit the sight screen.

'Try pitching it on the wicket,' suggested Jim.

'I am trying. Thanks,' I said.

Another couple of wides followed. The next ball I threw straight into the turf, just metres from my feet. It hit the ground with such force that it almost stopped dead, and then only trickled a few feet down the wicket. The rest of my team howled with laughter.

It was like I was having an out of body experience. I genuinely felt like I had no control over my arms and how fast to swing them, or when and how to release the ball from my grip.

'Just take it nice and slowly,' said Jim, between laughs. 'Just bowl a couple of slow ones to get you back in the groove.'

Even my slower ones rarely hit the wicket. I just wanted the over to be over, so that I could go and hide away at the boundary.

The problem with cricket is that although an over consists of six balls, balls that are bowled wide, too high, bounce too many times, or roll down the wicket, are illegal and don't count as one of the six. The batting team are also given an additional run for every 'wide' or 'no-ball' that is called. Occasionally, a ball of mine would be close enough for the umpire to leniently allow it. My first over consisted of 18 balls. That's 12 'extras' in one over. I slunk off to the boundary wishing the ground would swallow me up.

Three overs later, Tom approached me again.

'Fancy another chance?' he said, tossing me the cricket ball.

'You've got to be kidding? No way. That was one of the worst moments of my life.'

'It was just a blip. You must have got the yips. It happens to everyone at some point. You'll be fine if you try again. You've had some great overs in the past.'

'I don't want to bowl another cricket ball in my life.'

'Come on, that's not the right attitude. You've got to face your fears. Honestly, you'll be fine.'

'Alright,' I said. 'Just one more over.'

I didn't think my bowling could possibly get any worse. But somehow it did. It is all a bit of a blur, but I remember each ball being greeted by a combination of laughs, cheers and boos from our team, the two batsmen, the umpires, and the opposition team watching from the sidelines. They seemed to think I was doing it deliberately. My second over consisted of 21 balls, which is possibly a world record. The great Curtly Ambrose once bowled a 17-ball over. Pah! He was a loser compared to me.

Most of the balls that did make it to the other end of the wicket were so slow and crap that they were hit for four or six. It was *Walk On Stilts Day*, and if I had been wearing stilts at the time, it would not have been possible for me to bowl any worse. The opposition scored 55 from my two overs. 27 of those were 'extras', and therefore I finished as their highest run scorer. I am never going to play cricket again. Until next year, probably.

When I got home I built a pair of stilts using a broom, a mop, two bits of wood and some duct tape, to try and take my mind of the humiliation of the day. It worked for a while, and I was suitably amused and distracted by my creation, until I accidently snapped the mop in half and had to contend with Rachel's wrath too.

*For those unfamiliar with cricket, Graeme Swann went on to become an international cricketer for England. In 2009, he became the first English spin bowler to take 50 wickets in a calendar year. He was also a county cricketer for

Northamptonshire and Nottinghamshire. He is now a summariser for BBC's Test Match Special.

July 29th

Rain Day originated in the 1800s in Waynesburg, Pennsylvania. A farmer commented to pharmacist William Allison that it always rained on July 29th. William Allison began keeping a record of whether or not it actually rained on that date, and this continued for generations. News spread, and people started coming from further and further afield, to see it if it would rain in Waynesburg, Pennsylvania on July 29th. The celebrations expanded to include a pageant and other festivities.

The town celebrates regardless, but the festival is not considered a true success unless it rains. This year, there was no rain in Waynesburg.

But I damn sure celebrated on their behalf. I was photographing a Caribbean themed wedding in Milton Keynes. It was a clear, bright, sunny morning. The groom arrived at the church in an A-team van (as is traditional in the Caribbean, presumably) and then the heavens opened. It rained harder than it ever has at any wedding that I have photographed. It rained so violently during the ceremony that the vicar genuinely had to pause during her sermon because her voice could not be heard over the rain thundering the church's roof. It is no wonder that it stayed dry in Waynesburg; all of the sky's rain was being dumped onto Milton Keynes.

The bridal party all made a dash for their cars under a canopy of umbrellas and we drove the 30 minutes to the wedding venue. On our arrival, we were greeted by a steel band wearing floral patterned shirts playing in bright sunshine.

As if the celebration of *Rain Day* had not been enough, it was also *Lasagne Day*. The caterers clearly weren't celebrating and brought me a plate of Caribbean goat curry instead. It was particularly tasty, though, and far nicer than the microwaved lasagne that I ate when I got home later in the evening.

During a break in the wedding I had an answerphone message from the scary estate agent from Devon, so I called her back.

'Hello Mr Mahood,' she said sternly. 'We can offer you a viewing of the property but it would need to be tomorrow. Are you still interested?'

'Tomorrow... er... tomorrow might be a little short notice.'

'Well it's up to you. Other viewings have been scheduled for tomorrow, too, so if you leave it any later it might already be taken.'

'Tomorrow would be perfect. Thank you. What time?'

'Midday. Do you have the address?'

'Yes, we do. Thanks very much. Midday tomorrow it is.'

July 30th

It was the school summer holidays but we decided that it was not practical to take all three children to Devon and back in a single day. Even on a good day the journey takes four hours each way, and that's without any stops at all.

Fortunately, Rachel's parents were able to look after Leo and Kitty for the day. It was *Father-in-law Day*, so I celebrated this fleetingly with a quick cup of tea and a biscuit, before jumping into the car. We decided to take Layla with us, as we thought she might be a useful asset, and also, more importantly, she was desperate to bagsy the best bedroom.

We set off at 7am and the journey went smoothly until we were almost in Devon, when Layla, without warning, had a major nosebleed in the back of the car. I turned off the M5 at the next junction, and we pulled over to try and stop the bleeding. It was too late to avoid the massive bloodstains to her dress. So much for being an asset; we now had a bedraggled looking daughter with bloodstained clothing in tow.

'Are you nervous about seeing the house?' asked Rachel.

'Yes, very. Are you?'

'Very. What happens if we really like it but they offer it to someone else? Or what happens if the estate agent is even worse in real life than she was on the phone?'

'Exactly. And they would probably want to let it to other locals, rather than encouraging more out-of-towners like us to move into the area.'

We pulled up outside the farm on which the house was situated. It was even nicer than we imagined. We had been reluctant to live out in the middle of nowhere, but when we saw the location, thoughts of being close to the town centre instantly vanished. As we pulled into the farmyard another car was pulling out, with a young couple in the front.

'They've probably just looked at it, too,' said Rachel. 'I bet they've already signed the paperwork. There was no point in us even driving all of this way.'

'Let's both try to stop being so negative. I doubt they will have agreed anything before we've looked at it. They might not have even been looking at the house anyway,' I said, with a tinge of doubt.

We parked up in the farmyard and I soon spotted the house we had come to view; a beautifully converted barn, within a still operational stable block.

'It looks amazing,' I said to Rachel. 'Even better than in the photos.'

'Wow! Coooool. Are we going to live here?' asked Layla excitedly.

'We are only looking at the house for now. Lots of other people might want to live here, too,' said Rachel.

'Hello, can I help you?' asked a friendly voice from behind us.

'Hello. We've got an appointment to view this house at midday. Sorry, we are a little bit early.'

'Oh, not to worry. I'm Bill. My wife and I own the farm here.'

'Fantastic place you've got here, Bill,' I said. 'I'm George, this is my wife Rachel and this is our eldest daughter Layla.'

'Lovely to meet you all. Do you have any other children?'

'Yes,' said Rachel. 'Two others. A three year-old boy and a one-year-old girl.'

Rachel and I looked at each other and wondered whether this would count against us. Why would someone want to have three noisy young children moving into a house next door to them?

'Aw, that's great. We've got three grandkids, too. They live in our house with our daughter. I'm sure they would all get along smashing.'

Rachel and I smiled at each other and I ruffled Layla's hair and subtly adjusted her dress as best as I could to try and hide the bloodstain.

'Come on, let me show you around,' said Bill.

'What about Annie from the letting office?' I asked. 'Is she not coming?'

'No. We just used them to sort out possible tenants. We would be your landlords so you wouldn't be dealing with her again.'

'Thank god for that,' I whispered to Rachel.

Each room we walked through increased our excitement, but also built our feelings of nervousness and impending disappointment that this might be the only time we would set foot inside the building. There was so much more space than our house in Northampton. There was an additional bedroom, which meant I would no longer have to share my study with Kitty, chickens wandered around the garden, and from the kitchen sink you could see horses in the stable opposite. Washing up would no longer be a chore. Although, I decided not to tell this to Rachel.

Bill was a lovely man. He was in his early seventies, and spoke with a prominent Devon accent. He was born at the farm, as were his father and grandfather. He reminded me of Doug, in a comforting way.

His wife Sally joined us halfway through our tour and she was equally lovely. Layla was ridiculously animated to see the potential new house, and I had not seen her looking so happy in a long time. Rachel, on the other hand, was looking nauseous. I could tell she was worried about having our hopes dashed.

'So, what do you think?' asked Bill, once we were back in the kitchen.

Rachel and I looked at each other.

'We absolutely love it,' I said. 'I'm sure you've got lots of other people still to come and view it, but from our point-of-view, we are desperately keen, so please just let us know what you decide once you have completed all the viewings.'

'Well,' said Bill, looking at Sally, 'we would love you to move in.'

'Really?' squealed Rachel.

'Yes, really,' added Sally.

'Oh my god, that's fantastic. Do you mind if I give you a hug?' asked Rachel, who didn't wait for an answer and just grabbed hold of both Bill and Sally and squeezed them tightly. I joined them and we had a slightly awkward group hug in the kitchen.

'Well, that's that then,' said Bill. 'Why don't you come on over to the main house and we'll have a cup of tea and discuss all the details?'

'Sounds fantastic. Thank you,' I said.

Rachel and I gripped each other's hand tightly as we walked across the farmyard to Bill and Sally's house.

'Does that mean that we're going to live here properly?' asked Layla.

'Yes, I think so,' said Rachel. 'We've still got a few things to sort out but it looks like we will be allowed to move here.'

'That's AWESOME!' shouted Layla. 'Bagsy having the blue room.'

'We'll see,' I said.

We had a cup of tea and told Bill and Sally a little bit about ourselves, and learned a little about them. They were excited to hear that I was a wedding photographer and provisionally booked me to photograph their son's wedding at the local church in October. I had potentially got my first Devon booking and we hadn't even signed the letting agreement.

Bill said that he would speak to the agents, and Annie would be in touch to sort out contracts and deposits, and that he looked forward to us all moving down in the next few weeks. The whole thing felt very unreal.

As we sat in the harbour of the nearby town, eating fish and chips, surrounded by seagulls, with the waves lapping against the quay, it was a strange sensation knowing that there was now every chance that this would be our home town within a few weeks.

We finished our fish and chips and made a start on the long drive back up to Northampton. It was a drive I would soon be doing regularly, as all of my wedding bookings for the rest of the year and next, are predominantly in and around Northamptonshire. The plan was for me to start from scratch down in Devon and gradually build up work, whilst fulfilling my Northampton bookings.

As far as jobs go, moving to Devon was pretty much career suicide for me. Building up a steady income from photography was a long and arduous process, and just when things were starting to look after themselves, we decided to uproot and start again from the bottom. Financially it was a terrible decision, but if we were ever to make the move to Devon, then now - with only one of our three children settled in school - was undoubtedly the best time.

July 31st

To celebrate *National Recreation and Parks Month*, we decided to visit London Zoo with some friends. I know it's a very tenuous link. We had planned to go to the zoo, ok, and I needed to tie it into a holiday celebration somehow. It was also *Mutts Day*: a day to celebrate 'half-breeds'. Does a hyena count as a mutt? What about a jackal? Wolf? I'm sure London Zoo must have some mutts. Anyway, in my eyes, the zoo is one big park and recreation ground full of mutts. We were celebrating these holidays to the max.

We boarded the train to London, thinking it would be fun, stupidly forgetting that we would be sharing it with all of the London commuters. It turned out not everyone in the country was on their summer holidays.

Five of us shared two seats in a sweltering sauna of a carriage, and we tried to bribe the children into keeping quiet for the duration of the journey. We were unsuccessful and they whined the entire way there.

As we arrived at Euston my phone rang. It was Annie. I ushered Rachel ahead and said I would catch them up.

'Mr Mahood?' she said, in her manner as though she wanted to pick a fight.

'Hi Annie. How are you?'

'Fine. Now, I've heard from Bill and I gather they are happy for you to take on the tenancy.'

'Yes, that would be great, thanks.'

'Well don't get too excited just yet. There's lots more that we still need to discuss before we can agree to anything.'

'Right. Ok,' I said hesitantly. 'But I thought that Bill and Sally would be the landlords?'

'Yes, that's correct. Once the forms are signed then everything will be dealt with through them. But until that happens, we, as an agency, are responsible for ensuring that we get the best candidates to take on the tenancy.'

'Ok, but they seemed happy with the idea of us as tenants,' I said.

'That may be so, but I have a few concerns over your financial situation.'

'What sort of concerns?'

'Well, it says on the form that you are a photographer.'

'That's right.'

'And do you have regular work in the Devon area?'

'No, not at the moment. I will be driving back to Northampton regularly for work, but that's not a problem.'

'I see. And your wife? Does she have regular work in the Devon area?'

'No. She's a teacher and she'll be looking for work in the coming months.'

'So she is unemployed?'

'As of September, yes, but she'll hopefully pick up some work once we're down there.'

'I see.'

'I'm also an author,' I added reluctantly, 'so I get a bit of extra income from that.'

'How many books have you written?'

'Err.. well only one of them is published so far, but I'm just about to publish my second book, and I'm in the process of writing a third.'

'Congratulations,' she said, slightly sarcastically. 'Have you got a publishing deal for these books?'

'No. I published them myself.'

'Right,' she said, pausing for what felt like several minutes. 'You see, Mr Mahood, I am a little concerned that you might not be in the best situation financially to take on this tenancy. If, for example, a few months down the line you are unable to pay your rent, then the blame comes back to me.'

'Yes, I understand that you have a duty to the landlords, but I can assure you that we will meet all our payments.'

'It's easy for you to say that, Mr Mahood, but I don't think I will be able to proceed with this arrangement. There were other candidates who viewed the property and they were all in full-time employment.'

'I promise that we'll keep up-to-date with our rent,' I pleaded.

'Your word won't really be enough, I'm afraid.'

I felt a wave of sickness inside me, like a child whose ice-cream had just nose-dived into the gravel.

'How about...' I said, thinking on my feet '... if we pay six months rent up front?'

'Six months rent? Well... we don't normally do things like that.'

'I know, but if you have concerns about our ability to pay the rent, then we would be happy to pay six months rent up front.'

'Right, well, I will have to speak to the people who deal with the finances and give you a call back. You do realise that you also have to pay a month's rent as a deposit, so you would actually be paying seven months rent up front, plus all the fees of course.'

'Yes, that's absolutely fine,' I gulped.

'Right. I will talk to you later this afternoon.'

'I look forward to hearing from you later,' I lied.

I hurried after Rachel who had gathered with our friends outside Euston Station. We had agreed that we would all walk to London Zoo, rather than fight again with the commuters on the Underground.

'How on earth are we going to afford to pay seven months rent up front?' said Rachel, after I talked her through my conversation with Annie.

'I don't know. I can use the money that I put aside to pay my tax bill, and then I've got some savings I can use. I think I'll be able to scrape it together, just about.'

'But then how will you pay your tax bill? And will we have any money to live off?'

'We'll be fine. My tax bill doesn't have to be paid until next January, and our living expenses will be dramatically reduced as we won't have to pay any rent for six months. Besides, if I hadn't suggested it then there is no chance we would have got the house.'

'So is it definitely ours?'

'Not definitely. She is going to get back to me later.'

'Well done anyway. She's such an evil cow.'

We had an enjoyable day at London Zoological Park and Recreation Ground (to give it its full title), looking at a huge variety of mutts. I bought the children an ocarina to share from the gift shop to celebrate *Uncommon Instruments Awareness Day*. I should have learned from my mistake when I bought harmonicas for them on *Buy a Musical Instrument Day*. The journey home was even more unpleasant than the way down.

My phone rang on the train.

'Mr Mahood. It's Annie.'

'Hi Annie,' I said tentatively. 'So, what's the verdict?'

'Six months rent, plus the deposit and the fees will be fine. I will email over the tenancy agreement. If you can get it signed and transfer the money by the end of Friday, then you can have the keys to the house on August 9th.'

'We got it,' I said to Rachel.

It is impossible to sum up the look on her face, as she squeezed my knee in the crowded carriage.

AUGUST

August 1st

The issue of Father Dougal - our well loved, but slightly feral, cat - and our impending move had been playing heavily on my mind. Over years he started to spend more and more time at our neighbour's house, where he gets plenty of peace and quiet, and is fed extremely well.

It would be hard for Doug and Chris when we moved, but losing Father Dougal - or Basil, as they call him - would be even harder for them. I had been toying with the idea of leaving Basil in Northampton with Doug and Chris. Rachel wasn't so keen on the idea.

'But he's our cat,' she argued.

'I know. But he spends most of his time next door. We hardly see him anymore.'

'But if we moved house then he would be just our cat again.'

'Do you really think he wants to move house? He is very happy here. He has almost an entire house to himself next door with nobody to bother him.'

'I know, but it just doesn't seem right.'

'What about Doug and Chris? It's going to horrible for them when we leave, but what happens when they lose Basil too?'

'Maybe you're right. But imagine not having Father Dougal anymore.'

'But imagine Doug and Chris not having Basil anymore. At least we can come and visit him when we are back in Northampton. Doug and Chris would never see Basil again if he came with us to Devon.'

'That's true,' she said, pausing. 'Ok, I think you're right. It's probably for the best to leave him here. But what happens if Doug doesn't want to keep him?'

'I don't think there is any danger of that.'

To celebrate *World Wide Web Day*, I spent the day doing what I tend to spend far too much of my time doing - wasting time on the internet, mostly watching cat videos on YouTube. It's what Tim Berners-Lee invented the internet for.

August 2nd

We were a week away from getting the keys to the house in Devon, but there was still an awful lot to do. We found a removal company who were free on August 8th; they would load up the lorry and drive down to Devon that evening, ready to unload the following day.

There was a small problem, though. I had a wedding in Northampton on August 10th. We could not postpone the move because we had a holiday booked with a group of friends for the following week (ironically about four miles from where we were moving), so we decided to move our stuff down there, go on holiday, and then unpack when we got back.

I had to forget all about moving house today, and the millions of jobs to do, and go and photograph another wedding. The day was made more bearable when I called into the supermarket on the way home to purchase a selection of pale ales to celebrate *India Pale Ale Beer Day*.

August 4th

To try and get rid of some of the crap we had accumulated over the years, Rachel and I decided to do a car boot sale. It would have been a bad idea to take the children with us, as most of the crap we were selling was theirs. The grandparents were able to look after them, and Rachel and I set off early in two cars full to bursting.

We arrived at the popular car boot sale site in a local village at 6:30am, and were given a prime spot at the far end of the first row. As we parked our cars, scavengers surrounded us, squashing their faces up to the windows looking for early bargains. The official opening time for punters was not for another two hours. These were the dealers, and the real fanatics, who swarm on each new car and strip them of their valuables, before they have had a chance to set up.

I climbed out of my car and elbowed my way hastily through the hordes towards Rachel's car.

'Got any smartphones?'

'Got any electricals?'

'Any PlayStation games?'

'Any decent watches?' they said, clawing at me as I battled past. Rachel sat in her car with a look of panic on her face, as though she was about to witness me being torn to bits by the living dead. I was able to lip-read her through the windscreen over the commotion - 'What the fuck? Are you ok?'

I prised the passenger-side door open on Rachel's car and dived into the seat, before slamming the door, as the vacant expressions of the car boot sale zombies squashed their ugly faces up at the window.

'What is happening?' asked Rachel. 'Who are these people? It's like it's the end-of-the-world.'

'Don't worry. Just stay calm. It will all be over soon,' I said, with the calmness of a long in the tooth car boot sale professional. I had done a few car boot sales over the years and I knew the drill.

'Will it be like this the whole time?' said Rachel.

'No, we just have to sit it out.'

'But look at them!'

'Just ignore them. Don't make eye contact. It will only make things worse. If we get out the car now and start unloading they will have emptied the contents of the car before we've even got the table up.'

'So what do we do?'

'We wait. They'll soon get bored of us and move on to their next victims.'

The gormless faces continued to peer into the boot of the car. They showed no signs of dispersing.

After another five minutes, a small blue Ford Fiesta drove slowly past us and parked up to form the start of the next row. The gathered masses turned their heads and staggered off to their new victims. An elderly couple emerged from each side of the Fiesta as the scavengers surrounded them. You could see the shock and panic on the old couple's faces as they tried to fight off a barrage of questions from their attackers.

'That poor couple,' said Rachel. 'Look at them. They are being eaten alive. Should we do something to help?'

'It's too late. There is nothing we can do. We'll just have to leave them. It's every man for himself at this car boot sale.'

'Poor things. That could have been us.'

'I think we are safe to get out of the car now.'

We got our stall set up fairly quickly, and then the regular punters began to arrive. We were selling fairly well and there was a fair bit of interest in our stall. The clothes of Rachel's we had for sale seemed to be particularly popular amongst young, black teenage girls. She didn't know whether this was a compliment or not. Unsurprisingly, nobody seemed remotely interested in the few clothes of mine that we were selling.

A middle-aged man was delighted to purchase our VHS player for £2.50. After accepting his money, I double-checked that there was no video in the machine. I pushed back the flap and revealed the words '*George and Rachel - wedding video.*'

Our one and only copy of our wedding video, filmed by Rachel's uncle, was still in the machine and, as we had no power supply, there was no way to eject it. The video would have been in there for about nine years, since the machine went up into the attic. I reluctantly refunded the man his £2.50 and we were forced to put the VHS player back in the car.

I decided to help demonstrate some of the items that we had for sale. The first item that I tried on was a Mexican poncho, which I coupled with a bizarre cardboard face mask. I don't know why I thought it would increase our chances of sales. All it served to do was deter people from coming anywhere near our stall. I even made a young girl scream and go crying to her mummy. I then put on an inflatable rodeo bull costume that I had bought for a stag do a few years ago. It got a few laughs and comments from punters, but not enough to secure a sale.

Just as buyers started to congregate around our table in decent numbers - all thanks to my rodeo bull costume, I presume - it began to pour with rain.

'It's just a passing shower,' I said to Rachel, as I frantically covered any perishable items with plastic bags.

'It doesn't look like a passing shower,' she said, looking at the darkening sky that was enclosing us from every angle.

The punters all ran for their cars or the exit, and there was soon a queue of traffic trying to leave the football field on which the car boot sale was taking place.

Then all of the other stall-holders started to pack up, too.

'No point in hanging around,' said the man occupying the spot next to ours. 'I think that's it for the day. We'll try again next week.'

'What do you want to do?' asked Rachel.

'We might as well hang around for a bit to see if it dries up,' I said. 'We won't be coming back next week, so we should get rid of as much stuff as we can today.'

Half an hour later, we had reduced everything to 50p, and then offered to give everything away for free, but all of the other buyers and sellers had fled by this point, reluctant to take a chance on some now-soggy wares. We were the only people left in the entire field.

I was still standing there in my rodeo bull outfit, the bull dripping rain water from its nose. The hum of the battery-powered fan that kept it inflated whirred to a stop and the sodden costume deflated and slipped down my legs. I was a pathetic sight. Rachel had long since taken shelter in the car, and was reading her book in the warmth, whilst I clung to the notion that the rain would pass and the punters would return.

I now realised that this was more than a little unlikely.

I began to pack away all of our things, with the soggy rodeo-bull costume now around my ankles. I took it off and put the poncho back on for warmth whilst I loaded the car.

We sold £25 worth of stuff, which was not bad considering we only had customers for about 10 minutes. Unfortunately, we paid £12 for our two car pitches, and just before the gates officially opened, Rachel nipped off for a nose at other people's stalls and came back with four large sofa cushions, and a large wicker chest with a total combined cost of £18. We also bought a McDonald's breakfast on the way, at a cost of £6. This made an overall LOSS of £11, which is not, by anyone's standards, considered a successful morning.

Still, on the way home, we called into a charity shop and donated all of the clothes, books, and the children's toys. We then called into the tip where the rest of the contents of the car was disposed of, or recycled. All apart from the poncho, the VHS player, and the rodeo-bull outfit - which I had become quite attached to.

We came home with an almost empty car, and so, on that basis, the day had been a great success. Ironically, it was *National Kids' Day*, on a very rare day that Rachel and I had spent child-free.

We picked them up from their grandparents late afternoon and made the mistake of asking them what they wanted for dinner.

'McDONALD'S!' they all shouted in unison.

'Er.. but Mummy and Daddy have sort of already been to McDonalds today.'

'Oooh, that's not fair,' said Leo.

Rachel and I looked at each other.

'Ok then, McDonalds it is. It is *Kids' Day* after all.'

August 5th

'Morning Doug,' I said to him over the garden wall.

'Morning George. It's 68 degrees today,' he said, looking at the thermometer that hangs in his garden like he did several times a day.

'Is it? Wow,' I said, never quite sure whether that is considered cold, hot or average for the time of year. I don't understand the Fahrenheit scale at all, so it meant very little to me.

'I think I'll take a risk putting the washing out,' he said.

'Doug, Rachel and I were wondering if you would like to keep Father Dougal, sorry I mean Basil, when we move to Devon?'

'But he's your cat. Surely you'll be taking him with you, won't you?'

'Well we've had a talk about it and we think he would be much happier staying here with you.'

'I don't know about that, George' he said, his eyes watering slightly.

'We would miss him, of course, but I know he would be happier here than with us. He's got a life of luxury with you; no children to disturb him, lots of love and affection when he wants it, a nice warm house.'

'Well he certainly does get spoilt rotten. We'd feel so awful keeping him from you, though.'

'Please don't. It's honestly the best thing for everyone. So what do you think? Do you think Chris would be happy if he stayed here with you both?'

'I know it would mean the world to Chris. She was devastated when I told her you were all moving. I mean, obviously she will miss you, but she was particularly sad about losing Basil. No offence.'

'None taken,' I laughed. 'We know how important he is to you both. We feel so sad to be leaving Derby Road, and the thought of taking Basil away from you two is horrible.'

'But what about your other cat? Would she not miss him?'

'Are you kidding? He's a right bully. I don't think Batfink will miss him at all. So, is that a yes?'

'Well, if you're absolutely sure, then we would be delighted. Thanks, kiddo. I can't wait to go and tell Chris.'

'Thank you for looking after him. It gives us another excuse to come and visit you whenever we are back.'

Last Monday was *Pale Ale Day*, and according to my lists, today was *International Beer Day,* so I celebrated in style when I got home from my second consecutive Monday wedding. I don't make the rules.

August 6th

There were no spaces in Layla's year at the local school in Devon. We added her name to the waiting list as soon as we made the decision to move, and had also applied to several schools in the surrounding villages.

We received a call today from the local school. A space had opened up and did we still want it? We were all delighted by the news. All except Layla. She had originally been excited about moving house, as she loved the look of the blue room, the view of the horses, and the wandering chickens in the garden. She also loved the idea of moving closer to the beach. But that was all before the reality of it kicked in.

She was finding the whole thing very difficult, and was extremely upset about the idea of leaving her friends, her house, Doug and Chris, and Father Dougal. She resented us for moving, and it was hard to explain to her that it wasn't a selfish decision, and that we thought it would be best for all of us in the long run. We knew she would adapt very quickly, and it was definitely easier for her to move now than in a few years' time when she would be even more settled in school.

Colin, the removal man, confirmed that he and his men would come on Thursday to load up, and then unload in Devon on the Friday. That gave us two days to get everything sorted. As I had to be back in Northampton on Saturday, and as we weren't going to be unpacking the boxes until after our holiday, it was impractical for me to drive 250 miles there to help them unload the lorry, and then drive back to Northampton the following day.

We decided that it would be easier if I stayed put in Northampton until after the wedding, and then drive down for the start of our holiday on Sunday.

Equally, there was no point in Rachel and the children being in Northampton whilst the removal men loaded the lorry, as the three children would only inadvertently get in the way. We couldn't all stay until Sunday in Northampton, as the house would be completely empty. We agreed that Rachel and the kids would drive down to Devon before the removal men arrived, spend a few days at a holiday house with my parents, and supervise the removal men unloading the lorry that end.

And then I found £50.

August 7th

It was a somewhat poetic last day for us all in Northampton. It was *National Lighthouse Day*, and undoubtedly the most famous landmark in Northampton is the Express Lift Tower - or 'Northampton's Lighthouse', as Terry Wogan famously lampooned it. The NATIONAL Lift Tower, to give it its official title, is a 127m high tower that is used for testing lifts. It is the only building of its kind in the UK, and one of only two lift towers in Europe.

Seeing as it was *National Lighthouse Day*, we thought it appropriate to go and have one last look at it. Despite the children seeing it on almost every journey in Northampton they had ever been on, we had never actually gone and had a proper look at it. You can get a decent view of the tower from the beautifully picturesque spot that is the local recycling centre. We parked the car in a lay-by and stood and marvelled at the building, while the JCBs growled nearby, and the air was scented with decomposed rubbish.

'Why would they build a lighthouse here when we live so far from the sea?' asked Layla.

'It's not actually a lighthouse, it just looks like one,' I said. 'It's actually a lift tower. They use it to test lifts before they put them into other buildings.'

'Oh.'

'It opened in 1982 which was 31 years ago,' I said.

'But you're 34,' she said.

'Yes, that's right.'

'Wow, I've never met anyone that is OLDER than a building.'

Rachel burst out laughing and I for a moment suddenly felt incredibly old. The Lift Tower is Northampton's most recognisable landmark; it is what the town is known for. It is like it has always been there, yet I am older than it. It didn't feel right.

'I'm not THAT old,' I said.

'Yes you are. You're older than THAT,' she said, pointing to the tower. 'And THAT looks ancient.'

Rachel chuckled even louder. She was right, though. It did look ancient.

'I don't know what you're laughing at. You're two months older than I am,' I said to Rachel.

'Well maybe I don't look it,' she said.

On the way home, I took a detour into a brand new housing estate on the edge of town.

'How old are you, Layla?' I asked.

'Six. Why?'

'You see these houses? They are only one year old.'

'No they aren't.'

'Yes they are. They weren't here last year. I can't believe you are older than a building. I've never met anyone OLDER than a building.'

'Even Kitty is older than these buildings,' she said.

'Exactly.'

'But those are nice new shiny houses,' said Layla. 'You are older than that massive ugly grey lighthouse thing.'

'Alright, I think I've heard enough now. I get the message.'

August 8th

The house was pretty much packed up - which was a relief considering the removal men were on their way. It had all become too much for Layla and she suddenly got very cross and emotional.

'You don't care about me,' she shouted. 'You are just moving for no reason. Why would you do that?'

'We are not moving for no reason. We are moving to a nicer house, in a lovely part of the country, and you will really love it there, I promise,' I said.

'But all of my friends are here,' she said, through the tears.

'I know, but they can come and visit and you can come back and visit them, and you can write to them and talk on the phone.'

'It's not the same. Why are you doing this? It's so unfair!'

'It does seem unfair, but I promise that in a few weeks you will be so happy in your new house, and your new school.'

'But I like it here. And what about Father Dougal?'

'Father Dougal is going to stay and live with Doug and Chris, because he's happier here.'

'But he's OUR CAT,' she shouted. 'I want him to live with US.'

'We will come and visit him, too.'

'That's not the same. He's our cat. I'll miss him.'

'We'll all miss him, but he wouldn't like moving to Devon. He'll be much happier here.'

Ironically it was *International Cat Day*. I didn't tell Layla this, as I didn't think it would have helped the situation. It was also

Sneak Some Zucchini Onto Your Neighbour's Porch Night, so later that night I did, which was a little weird.

We loaded the car with the bags that Rachel needed for the next few days, and we went to say goodbye to Doug and Chris. I was going to be at the house for another three nights, but it felt like this was the proper goodbye.

When we moved into our house nearly eleven years ago, I had no idea that the slightly strange looking man next door, who walked around in a vest, singing obscure music hall songs, would become such a big part of our lives.

'So, this is it, is it?' said Doug.

'Yes, me and the kids are about to head off now,' said Rachel, wiping away a tear.

'Chris and I are going to miss you all so much. It's not going to be the same without you,' said Doug.

'We are going to miss you so much,' said Rachel. 'We promise we'll keep in touch and will make sure we come and visit.'

'You are welcome any time.'

I was standing to one side while Rachel did the talking. I didn't think I would feel too emotional saying goodbye, especially as I wasn't even leaving, but the enormity of the whole thing suddenly hit me and I started to sob.

'Come here, kiddo,' said Doug, wrapping his arms around me and squeezing me tightly.

We strapped Layla, Leo and Kitty into their car seats ready for their drive down to Devon. This would be the longest I had ever gone without seeing the children and it was a very odd feeling.

'Drive carefully,' I said to Rachel, giving her a kiss and hugging her close.

'I will. I hope it all goes ok with the removal men.'

'I'm sure it will all be fine. And you guys all behave yourselves,' I said, leaning in to the back of the car and planting a kiss on each of their foreheads.

'We will,' they all said.

'Be good to Mummy. She is going to report back on how well you've behaved, OK?'

'Okaaaay,' they sighed. Layla was still scowling, but the tears had stopped.

'You'll love living in Devon,' I whispered. 'Just you wait and see.'

Doug and I watched as Rachel manoeuvred the car in her trademark seven point turn to get it facing the other way down the street.

'Golly, I'll miss watching her parking from our window. It's the highlight of my day,' he laughed.

'See you in a few days!' I called, as Rachel beeped the horn and the car soon disappeared from view.

The removal men arrived 15 minutes later and we made an immediate start on the loading. I offered to lend a hand and they were happy for the additional help. The four of us had the lorry loaded in just a couple of hours, punctuated with frequent stops for tea and biscuits.

It was *Happiness Happens Day*. Originally founded in 1999 by the *Secret Society of Happy People* (I am not making any of this shit up), it's a day to promote and celebrate happiness.

I felt a mixture of emotions, but happiness was buried far below the surface. I was sad that I wouldn't see Rachel, Layla, Leo or Kitty for four days. I was anxious about the move and the jobs I had over the coming days. I was scared about the prospect of starting anew in terms of work and friends. I was excited about the adventure and a new start, and underneath all of that, I hoped that happiness would flourish soon afterwards.

The house was completely empty apart from me, Batfink the cat, an airbed, my camera bag and a few clothes. All love and feeling had been stripped from the house and it was no longer our home but just a shell. It didn't feel emotional spending time under that roof because all of our possessions had moved on to our new beginning, and all of the happy memories would stay with us, wherever we lived.

It felt very lonely being in the house on my own, when I wanted nothing more than to be down in Devon ready to begin our new life.

I went and ordered a shish kebab and chips from Embers Grill takeaway, just like the good old days. It would, in all likelihood, be my last from Northampton. I no longer had my loyalty card, having weaned myself off kebabs after Rachel accused me of being 'biggishly built', but if I still had a loyalty card, I would have handed in it to the staff as a symbolic act of resignation.

It was a particularly hot evening, so I sat in my pants on the airbed, alone in an echoey house, with the patio doors wide open, and drank a bottle of wine as I stared at the empty walls.

August 9th

At some point I must have passed out. I woke in the morning to heavy banging on the door at 7:30am. I hastily pulled on a t-shirt and some trousers and opened the door to find Doug standing there looking quite worried.

'Morning Doug,' I said. 'Everything ok?'

'Yes, sorry for knocking so early. I just wanted to make sure you were alive.'

'Err... yeah... I think I am, just about. Why?'

'Well I was worried about you last night. Your patio doors were open and I could see you lying on the airbed half-naked. I tried shouting to you, but there was no response. I was worried you were dead.'

'Oh, sorry about that. I must have just been in a very deep sleep.'

'Right you are. Had you had a bit too much of the old grog?' he said, mimicking a googly eyed person drinking from a bottle.

'What? No, I only had a glass or two of wine.'

'Well, I'm glad you're ok. When you've had a chance to get yourself sorted, come round and I'll cook you a fry-up.'

'That's very kind of you but there's no...'

'It's non-negotiable. I insist.'

'Ok, then. Thanks.'

'Do you know anything about the courgettes on our doorstep?'

'Courgettes? No, nothing to do with me,' I said.

Doug is a vegetarian (that's not why I left him the courgettes, by the way), but he's one of those vegetarians that eats sausages, ham and bacon. And most other meats, in fact. He does go through phases of not eating much meat, so he feels that he still fits into the category of vegetarian.

After a very enjoyable breakfast, I had another photography job at the Carlsberg brewery (other beers are available). The Northampton Saints rugby team are sponsored by Carlsberg and were given their first ever tour of the brewery, followed by a free drinking session at the bar. If Carlsberg did photography jobs... oh, wait.

I spoke to Rachel on the phone and the removal lorry had made it down to Devon, but it had not been without incident. Bill, our new landlord, had advised Rachel to give the drivers specific instructions on how to get to the house avoiding the extremely narrow roads. Rachel had tried her best, but the removal men had insisted they were fine and they would find the house using sat nav.

First of all they were directed up a narrow one-way street which was lined with cars. They had to knock on doors of several houses for cars to be moved so that they could squeeze past. They then managed to get the lorry stuck in the mud bank on one of the tight corners. They had to dig the lorry out with shovels, and then physically widen the turning circle of the bend. Part of the lorry's front bumper snapped off in the process of getting it round. They apparently took this all in remarkably good spirit.

Colin parked up the lorry by the house and Rachel offered them a lift into the nearby town, and gave them some extra money for beers and food. The plan was for them to get a taxi back to their lorry, where they would sleep in the cab.

At 11:30pm Rachel had a text from Colin.

'Can't remember where the house is.
What's the address please?'

I had dinner over at a friend's house and returned for another night on my deflated airbed. With an absence of any other furniture in the entire house, Batfink had decided to use the airbed to sharpen her claws. Airbeds and cat's claws are not a good combination. Father Dougal also made an appearance in the middle of the night. He sprinted around the house, meowing his head off (not literally), clearly a bit freaked out by the change in his surroundings. He then sprayed urine on the airbed and disappeared out the cat flap back to Doug's house.

81

I decided that the airbed now had very little in the way of redeeming features, as it was no longer full of air, and now coated in cat piss, so I opted to sleep on the hard wooden floor instead.

August 10th

I left the house early and spent the day photographing a wedding. I returned in the evening and half-heartedly watched some Duran Duran videos on YouTube. It was *Duran Duran Appreciation Day*, by the way. I'm not THAT odd.

I then badly toasted some marshmallows on the gas hobs and stuck them between two digestives with a piece of Dairy Milk. It was also *S'mores Day* - the American campfire tradition of toasted marshmallows and chocolate, sandwiched between two pieces of Graham cracker. My version was not quite faithful to the original recipe but it was the best I could do under the circumstances. It still tasted pretty damn good.

S'mores, I imagine, are best enjoyed in a group around a campfire, rather than alone on a gas hob.

August 11th

I woke on the hard wooden floor on what would be my last morning in Northampton. Doug invited me over for another of his 'vegetarian' fry-ups and I then spent a couple of hours cleaning the house before loading my few possessions into the boot of the car. My passenger for the 4.5 hour journey was Batfink in her cat carrier on the front seat.

It was staggering to think of everything that had happened since Rachel and I had bought our first house together 11 years ago. We moved in as an unmarried couple, working in badly paid temping jobs. This house has seen us get engaged, get married, have three children (two of them born IN the house), have pets, go through several jobs, Rachel's teacher training, parties, arguments, laughs, tears, and creating eleven years of amazing memories.

It was just a house.

A pile of bricks and mortar.

But it has been the venue for so many of the key events in our lives. No other house that we live in will ever be able to match the significance that it has had.

But I didn't feel any real emotion towards the house. I took one last tour, pausing only briefly in each empty room, and taking it all in. I thought I would find it hard locking the front door for the very last time and knowing that I wouldn't be back. But I was ready. The time felt right.

'So long, Derby Road. Thanks for all the memories,' I said to myself as I pulled the front door to, and heard the familiar click of the latch as it locked.

Saying goodbye to Doug and Chris was far more difficult.

'So this is it,' said Doug. 'What can I say? I don't know what we'll do without you.'

'You've been the best neighbours for the last 11 years,' I said. 'But we'll keep in touch, and you'll be seeing plenty more of us, you can be sure of that.'

'Do you promise to come and visit?'

'Of course I will. I've still got lots of work in Northampton for the rest of this year and next, and I'll come and see you whenever I'm up. In fact, we will all be back for a friend's wedding at the end of this month.'

He squeezed me tightly.

'And I know you'll take great care of Basil,' I said, picking up Father Dougal and giving him a big cuddle too. He started purring which was a rarity in recent years. It was almost as though he knew what was happening. Or more likely, he was hungry and hoping that I would feed him.

'Take care, kiddo. And don't forget about us,' said Doug, leaning through the car window.

I started the engine and set off down the road. I gave the horn a double-beep and waved my hand out of the window. I watched in my rear-view mirror as Doug stood on the pavement until I had reached the end of the street.

It was *Ingersoll Day*; a day to commemorate Robert Ingersoll - one of the most important freethinkers in US history. No offence to Robert, but I didn't care a rat's arse about him today. It was also *Son and Daughter Day*, and that was far more important to me. Although it had only been three and a half days, it was the longest I had been without seeing my son and daughter(s), and I was desperate to see them and Rachel. Today was the start of a brand new adventure; one that I was beginning with the rest of my family, and I couldn't wait to get started.

Batfink was less enthusiastic and howled like a wolf the entire way to Devon.

We had booked a week's holiday at a little house that I have been staying at since I was an infant. The day we finished our A-levels, a group of my school friends went for our very first grown-up-free holiday, and we have been every summer since. The numbers have dwindled over the years, as people have got married, got more demanding jobs, had children or decided that the accommodation is a little rustic for their taste. It's very basic; the toilet is not in the house, the floors are made of stone and very cold, the bedding is always damp and slightly mouldy, and the kitchen is only big enough for one person at a time. But its location, just a stone's throw from the beach and the river estuary, is particularly special.

The house sleeps six people comfortably, and seven or eight at a push. At its peak, we crammed 24 people into that tiny house and garden for a week. Most people slept in tents, and food was cooked on the barbecue - three meals a day - to avoid overcrowding the kitchen.

This year, there were seven of us; the five of our family, plus two friends from Northampton. They all arrived on Friday and I eventually arrived mid-afternoon on Sunday.

It felt strange knowing that all of our possessions were sitting in boxes at our new house just four miles away, but it was also comforting that we didn't have to worry about any of it for a few days and could just enjoy the holiday.

Poor old Batfink had to come on holiday with us, too. I let her out of the cat carrier, she took a quick sniff around the place and then disappeared under a sofa where she spent most of the following week, reappearing very occasionally to eat or use the litter tray.

August 12th

Leo is our middle child and today was *Middle Child Day*. It's a chance to recognise that the middle child is often neglected. The first child is always the first child; that's where all the initial love, affection and wonder at having a newborn baby is directed. The youngest child of three will always be the baby of the family; perhaps slightly more vulnerable than the others, and therefore doted on more. The middle child doesn't fit these criteria, so often languishes somewhere in the middle.

I think that because Leo is our only boy, he has found his own role, though. This makes him unique and hopefully he'll have avoided any Middle Child Syndrome.

I celebrated the holiday anyway, and had a couple of hours on the beach just with Leo. We played football, flew a kite, and got an ice-cream. Did some shit that boys do.

August 13th

Today was Layla's day. It was *Lefthander's Day,* and as the only lefthander in the family, it was only fair to spend some quality time just with her. We went shopping for shoes, painted our nails, and watched a chick flick. Did some shit that girls do.

August 14th

Not wanting Kitty to feel left out, I had to try and incorporate one of today's celebrations into some quality time with her. Unfortunately for Kitty, today's holidays didn't adapt too favourably into children's entertainment. *Victory Over Japan Day* is the anniversary of the date on which Japan surrendered, ending World War II. It was also *National Navajo Code Talkers Day,* which celebrates the role that Native-Americans played in both world wars, using their native languages to transmit messages securely across the airwaves. Kitty was in for a real treat.

We talked in code, read some history books, did some shit that one-year-olds do.

August 15th

'When are we going to go to our new house?' asked Leo.

'Soon. When we've finished our holiday,' I said.

'But when? I want to go to our house now.'

'Aren't you having a nice holiday?'

'Yes, but I really want to go and see what my new bedroom looks like.'

'I already know what it looks like,' boasted Layla. 'But I do want to see it again.'

We had a great few days and the weather had been kind, but today, however, it turned miserable. It had been nice to just switch off, but in the back of our minds, both Rachel and I were itching to get into our new house and start unpacking. It was less than 10 minutes away from where we were staying, yet I hadn't even seen the house since the day we came to view it. Leo and Kitty hadn't seen it at all. The wet weather meant that we were all cooped up inside the small house, but we weren't due to leave until the following day.

It was *National Relaxation Day*, and I felt that neither Rachel nor I were relaxing completely when we wanted to be elsewhere. I suggested to our two friends that they come back and have a look at it and they jumped at the chance of a change of scenery.

We spent the rest of the afternoon assembling bunk beds, unpacking kitchen things, and making up the beds. It already started to look like our home. All of our possessions from our old house were now transplanted into a new building. Because that's how moving house works, in case you didn't realise.

August 17th

Back in June I tried (and failed) to start a Northampton letterboxing movement - a series of clues leading to carefully hidden plastic boxes. I then read about the sport of Geocaching, but decided that neither me nor Northampton were quite ready for GPS. Well today was *International Geocaching Day,* so it was time for me to get with the times. Geocaching, in case you don't know, is a recreational activity using a Global Positioning System receiver - such as a smartphone - to track down hidden containers that usually house a log book and stamp. It is basically orienteering for the 21st century.

I heard other dads claiming that their kids loved Geocaching, so thought it only fair that I give it a go, too. I downloaded a free Geocaching app onto my phone and logged on. To my surprise, there were many locations detected in the local area; a couple within a mile of our house.

Rachel was busy unpacking boxes, so I offered to take the children out for a few hours to give her a bit of space, and mostly because I was bored of unpacking already. I'm not very good at unpacking. I open a box, get something out, and if I don't immediately know what it is, or where it lives, I put it back and move on to the next box. This annoys the hell out of Rachel who meticulously works her way through each box, making sure every single item finds a home before moving on to the next.

'Right, so it says there is a location 100 yards from here,' I said, staring at the data on my phone while standing in the middle of a field.

'Can we hold your phone, Daddy?' said Leo.

'I suppose so. But you have to be really careful with it, ok? I don't want you dropping it in any puddles.'

'We won't,' said Leo, in a voice like it's the hundredth time I've told him.

'The arrow is pointing this way. Let's go,' said Layla.

'This way!' shouted Kitty, tagging along behind.

We followed a track to a gate, and then into some woodland.

'It's up in these bushes,' said Leo.

'Well done. Go and see if you can find it,' I said. 'I'll wait here by the path.'

I watched as the three of them climbed their way into a bush and then I heard shouts of: 'We've found it. We've found the treasure.'

I had perhaps hyped it up too much by describing it as 'treasure'. It was in fact just a rubber stamp for them to stamp onto a piece of paper.

'But where's our treasure?' asked Layla. 'That wasn't treasure.'

'Well it was, sort of. You had to follow a map to find it.'

'But we didn't get to keep anything.'

'You can have a treat when we get home.'

As we were walking back through the fields I checked my pocket to retrieve my phone and noticed it was missing.

'Leo, what did you do with my phone?'

'Oh. I think we left it in that bush. Sorry.'

'What did I tell you? That was silly. Let's go back and get it.'

We retraced our steps into the woods.

'Can you remember which bush it was?' I asked.

'No. Look at your phone and it will tell us,' said Leo.

'You left my phone in the bush!'

'Oh yeah. Oops!' he laughed.

After about five minutes of searching we found it sitting in some mud inside a bush. I wiped it down and it appeared to be functioning correctly.

'Who wants to find some more treasure?' I asked.

'MEEEE!' they all said.

'Ok, but I'm holding the phone this time.'

Meaning of 'Is' Day was created in recognition of President Bill Clinton's testimony during the Monica Lewinsky trial. Clinton responded to one of the questions with: *'It depends upon what the meaning of the word 'is' is'*, and somebody has since turned this day into a holiday celebration.

It was unclear how I was supposed to celebrate it. Rachel had given herself the role of my Administrative Assistant during this challenge, but unfortunately she wasn't willing to play Monica Lewinsky.

I also treated myself to a selection of 'new' clothes, bought from the local charity shops in celebration of *National Thrift Shop Day*. I'm quite a catch. Rachel is one very lucky lady.

August 18th

One of the first ways in which we noticed that life in Devon was different to Northampton, was with the postman. Our Devon postman is a nice guy (not a patch on Jason our Northampton postman, obviously) but his methods are very different. The door with our letterbox on is accessed via a small gate and a walk of about five metres. This was obviously too much of an inconvenience for the postman, so instead he just piles the mail on the step by the other door.

This morning it was raining, and I was in the shower. I came downstairs and found our mail on the side in the kitchen. Rather than walking the five metres to the letterbox, and not wanting the letters to get wet, the postman had just let himself in through the other door instead.

Jason, our Northampton postman, and I have become 'friends' on Facebook. He sent me a message asking how we were getting on, and I replied and told him about our new postman leaving our mail on the side in the kitchen.

'Imagine if I did that in Northampton,' he said. 'I don't think they'd take too kindly to that.'

Amongst the pile of junk mail that greeted me was a catalogue for an online gardening store. Usually I put these straight into the recycling bin before Rachel has a chance to see them, but today was *Mail Order Catalogue Day*, so I didn't have a choice but to look at it.

It was also *(World) Daffodil Day*. The daffodil has become a symbol for many different cancer charities around the world. The Australian organisation *Cancer Council* created *Daffodil Day* as a specific day to fundraise. I made a donation to a cancer charity and ordered some daffodils from the mail-order catalogue.

Do I know how to party, or what?

August 24th

As if Batfink had not suffered enough in recent weeks, she now had to be shipped off to her fourth 'home' in two weeks. She had spent her entire life, since being a kitten, at our house in Northampton, where she rarely strayed further than our garden wall. Then we took her on holiday with us, she then spent a week in our new house, and now she was going to spend a week in a cattery for the very first time, while we went to Wales for a week.

We all piled into the car and drove for five hours to the holiday house we were going to be staying in with Rachel's family. Rachel's parents had hired a giant farmhouse, built in 1394, for us all.

'This house is much older than the Express Lift Tower,' I said to Layla as we walked through the front door.

'Well it doesn't look that old.'

'It's over 600 years old!'

'Wow, that's even older than you.'

The house was a rabbit warren of rooms, corridors and stairways full of an eclectic mix of furniture and pictures from every era of its 600 year history. It was the sort of house that, had it not been filled with 12 people, would have felt quite spooky.

Rachel's sister and brother-in-law inadvertently celebrated one of the holidays for me on the first night. At about 2am in the morning, we awoke to banging from their room above ours. There was a few seconds of silence followed by frantic pounding footsteps, causing the lamp in our room to swing. Then silence again. Then a yelp from Rachel's sister, followed by the footsteps again, this time covering the entire perimeter of the room. A few more shrieks followed, and then another bout of the running.

'What on earth is going on up there?' I said to Rachel.

'Dunno,' said Rachel, still half asleep.

'Should I go and see if they're ok?'

'No. They'll be fine,' she muttered. 'Go back to sleep.'

After about 30 minutes the noise eventually stopped and I drifted back to sleep.

August 25th

Over breakfast we learned that Rachel's sister had woken in the night to something flapping past her face. She turned the light on and discovered a large bat flying circuits around the room. Getting rid of the bat was a 'man's job' apparently, so

Eric had to spend half an hour doing his own laps of the bedroom trying to coax the thing out of the window with a towel.

It kept coming to rest in inaccessible places, and then setting off again, and Rachel's sister wasn't willing to turn the light off until it was officially out of the bedroom. Eric had eventually managed to shepherd it towards the chimney, and it made its escape, presumably the same way it had got into the room. He then blockaded the fireplace with a chair, suitcases and pillows, before draping towels over the construction to prevent any further intruders.

Purely coincidentally, the night of August 24th is *International Bat Night*. I am honestly not making this up. It could just as easily have been Rachel and I that slept in the top room, and we could have celebrated *Bat Night* first hand. Or should that be first wing.

Rachel is easily traumatised by any flying creature and if she had been the one to wake up to a bat flying over her head, the holiday would have been over before it had even started.

August 29th

Edmond Hoyle was a writer in the 18th century, best known for publishing books detailing the rules of particular card games. He began with *A Short Treatise on the Game of Whist*, and followed that up with books about chess, backgammon and other card games. The phrase *'According to Hoyle'* came into use as a way of proving authority over a subject. At first, just with the games on which he was a published expert, but it then spread into other aspects of life.

My family have always played a lot of games - especially card games - and my dad is always in charge of the rules. He will often voice an opinion of a particular rule or method: 'THEY *say you should never lead with a seven or an eight,*' or 'THEY *say that you should always discard any low-scoring hearts first.*' I always go along with it, accepting that THEY must be an authority on the subject, despite secretly thinking '*who the fuck are THEY?*' It no longer matters, because now I have Hoyle.

August 30th

I didn't take my holiday celebrating too seriously during the week, as I wanted to be able to enjoy the holiday for what it was. Also, I still am not openly celebrating these holidays so it's difficult to explain why I would crumble up a cracker and sprinkle it all over my laptop's keyboard to celebrate *Crackers Over the Keyboard Day.* And how would I explain why I was moving my mouse around so frantically to try and celebrate *Race Your Mouse Around the Icons Day*? I did both of these, but I did them in private.

August 31st

One of the disadvantages of photographing weddings is that on beautiful summer days I have to watch people drinking nice cold beers in the sunshine, while I work. Today was the wedding of my friend Jim, and I was there as a guest. I had not been a guest at a wedding for 18 months.

It would be a vast understatement to say that I took advantage of being allowed to drink. I was very, very drunk. Thankfully, not so drunk that I was sick or unable to walk - although that probably would have been preferable for everyone else. I was quite the opposite - I had far too much energy.

I had been snacking on a bag of Trail Mix secretly stashed in my suit pocket (it was *National Trail Mix Day*). During the speeches, the best men told the story about Jim's pathetic attempt at a Guinness World Record waffle eating attempt, when he managed a feeble two waffles in 10 minutes. They provided Jim with a plate piled high with waffles as a memento and a visual aid for their speech. Following a three-course meal, I then ate two pizzas that were served from a pop-up pizzeria in the evening. I later stumbled upon the plate of waffles on one of the tables. Despite being completely stuffed, I thought it would be rude not to attempt a waffle eating contest. I tried to encourage others to join me, but they all sensibly declined, due to an obscene amount of food and drink already consumed. Not to be discouraged, I decided to attempt it on my own. I managed an impressive five waffles in ten minutes, but I felt as though my insides were going to rupture and spill the contents of my guts all over the wedding marquee. Fortunately they didn't, and I chose to ease the discomfort by taking part in an MC Hammer *'Can't Touch This'* dance-off... with myself. And to make matters worse, I certainly lost. Despite my drunken state, I can clearly picture Rachel's mortified face on the edge of the dance floor as I attempted to lasso her with my imaginary rope.

I am yet to see any mobile phone camera footage so I'm hoping I escaped. It was a top wedding, though, and a brilliant day.

It was refreshing not to have a camera with me either, as there is always the temptation to be snapping away. I took one photo during the entire day, with my mobile phone. It was a photo of a bridesmaid - the bride's sister - doing an involuntary power slide at the bride's feet on the dance floor. I don't even remember taking it, but it's comforting to know that there was someone at the wedding more drunk than me.

SEPTEMBER

September 1st

Rachel kindly offered to drive us back down to Devon, as I was feeling a little worse for wear. We called in to see Doug, Chris, and Basil before leaving Northampton, and there was a strange sense of déjà-vu as we pulled away from our old house. This time it felt different. We were driving back down to Devon which was now our home. Although, rather depressingly, in less than a week's time, I would be driving back up to Northampton for work.

There is an iconic statue that stands on the roof of a building on North Figueroa Street in Los Angeles, which forms part of the historic Route 66.

The 22-foot tall statue is of a man with a chicken's head clutching a bucket of fried chicken. He is affectionately known as *'Chicken Boy'*.

The statue was an installation for a nearby fried chicken restaurant up until the death of the restaurant owner in 1984. The statue was then given to Amy Inouye, a local art director, who kept the statue in storage for 20 years, before having it installed on the roof of her design firm's new premises. Some people refer to him as *The Statue of Liberty of Los Angeles. Chicken Boy's Day* is celebrated on September 1st each year in his honour.

We celebrated how Chicken Boy would have wanted - with some fried chicken, of course, from a service station on the M5.

September 3rd

'Mummy, Daddy have you seen the new kittens in the yard?' shouted Layla as she ran into the kitchen.

'What new kittens?' I said.

'Fred and Rocky. Sally bought them as a present for her grandchildren.'

'Really? Where are they?'

'Just wandering around outside. Come and look.'

We followed her outside and two of the cutest kittens I had ever seen, were chasing each other around the farmyard near our front door.

'Should they be out like that? Do you think they escaped somehow?' said Rachel.

'No, they don't live in the house,' said Layla. 'Sally bought them to be farm cats to catch mice and things.'

'How do you know?'

'She told me.'

'Do they get fed?'

'Yes, she leaves food out for them. Can we play with them?'

'Yes, I should think that's fine. Just be careful with them. Remember they are only little and not as tough as Batfink.'

Despite moving to house that was significantly bigger than the one we had in Northampton, and despite getting rid of a lot of stuff on the day of the car boot sale, we had still somehow managed to fill our new house.

It was *Another Look Unlimited Day*; a day when you are encouraged to take a second look around the house and find items that are no longer needed, and, rather than take them to a landfill, donate them to charity or up-cycle them in some way. Layla and Kitty both had birthdays in the last couple of months, which meant an increase in the amount of shit we

97

owned. We spent a couple of hours sorting through the toys and bagged up any that had not been used for some time (by 'we', I mean Rachel). Needless to say, Layla, Leo and Kitty spotted a plastic toy poking out of the top of one of the bin bags.

'Mummy, why are all of these toys in a bin bag?' asked Leo.

'Err, we were just having a bit of a sort out,' said Rachel.

'You weren't going to get rid of them were you?' she questioned.

'No! Of course not.'

'Then why are they in a bin bag?'

'We just put them in there so you could have a look through them. We noticed you hadn't played with them for a while.'

'Thanks. These are all my favourite ever toys,' she said, decanting the entire bag onto the kitchen floor.

We might have failed in the decluttering, but there is no better way to give the children a new appreciation for their neglected toys, than by attempting to get rid of them.

September 4th

It was Layla's first day at school. She is an incredibly brave girl and doesn't get too upset about things like this. She had no problem starting nursery and moving on to 'big school', but this was different. She had grown familiar with all of her peers in Northampton, having moved through nursery and the school years with the same group of children. She was now going to move into a class in which she knew absolutely nobody. She tried her best not to show it, but it was clear that she was nervous. So were Rachel and I. We were also used to the familiar faces at school drop-off, and it was going to be a strange transition to try and integrate into a new school life for all of us.

Leo started pre-school, too. Although slightly reluctant when we dropped him off, he was extremely positive when we picked him up at lunchtime.

Layla was full of smiles at the end of the day, too, and reeled off a list of all her new best friends, and talked incessantly the whole way home about all of the amazing things that her new school had. It transpired that last year her class had all spent a day out at the farm on which we live.

'Wow! You live on Farmer Bill's Farm? That's sooo cooool.'

'Do you have to feed all the animals?'

'Do you get to ride the horses?'

'Do you drive a tractor?'

'Do the sheep keep you awake at night?'

'Do you have fresh eggs for breakfast every day?'

She had become the new class celebrity.

September 5th

There is a lot of pressure in modern society to stick to timings. Our routines are governed by schedule, and the requirement to get to a specified place, at a precise time, to do a particular thing. Today was a day to embrace bad time-keeping. Today was *Be Late For Something Day*; a chance to say *'fuck you'* to schedule and routine. The problem is, I hate being late. I often am late, particularly when doing things with three children, but I still find it stressful, especially if it means I am letting people down.

I was due to take Kitty to her first mums and tots session in our new town. I have done my fair share of baby groups over the years, and I have never found them particularly pleasurable.

As a dad, I am always in the minority. On the rare occasion that there is another dad present, we will both stand in opposite corners of the room, alternating between playing trains with our child, and staring at our phones and avoiding eye contact with other parents. There is only one thing more socially awkward than a dad at a mums and tots, and that's two dads at mums and tots.

I do chat to other mums occasionally, but I know they are only talking to me out of sympathy, and would probably much rather be talking to other mums.

The group was due to start between 9:45am and 10am. In order to be late, I arrived like a badass at 10:15am.

'Hello, Kitty!' said the first lady we saw.

How did they know Kitty? This was her first time.

'Hi Kitty. How are you?' said another lady, as we hung our coats on the peg.

'Hello. You must be Rachel's husband,' said a lady, as though she had been expecting me.

'Yes. I'm George. Nice to meet you. Sorry we're late,' I said.

'Not at all. People come and go as they chose. I'm Sarah. Let me show you around and introduce you to everyone.'

It turned out that almost everyone at the group had already met Kitty and Rachel at the school gates; most of them had older children at school with Layla. I was astounded - in just a couple of days, Rachel already knew most of the town.

As expected, I was the only dad present, but all of the mums were extremely welcoming and I didn't feel awkward in the slightest.

Being late for something wasn't so bad after all.

September 8th

I arrived home at 2am after a busy 24 hours in Northampton, photographing a wedding, and a brief visit to see Doug beforehand. I was woken in the morning by excited children at 6:30am.

'Daddy's home!' they said.

'Yes, I am. Did you miss me?'

'Yes. Can you log on to the computer for us to play Deadly Dash. Mummy can't remember the code,' said Leo.

'Oh, is that why you missed me?'

'Yes. Why did you think?'

'Oh, no reason.'

It was *National Grandparent's Day*. I no longer have any grandparents, but we phoned Rachel's granddad Walter who was delighted, and slightly confused to be wished a Happy Grandparent's Day. He was probably a bit annoyed that nobody had celebrated it for the other 36 years of being a grandparent.

September 9th

September 9th is *Wonderful Weirdoes Day*. Purely coincidentally, it is also both my mum's and Rachel's mum's birthdays. I am not suggesting there is any correlation between them and *Wonderful Weirdoes Day*. I just thought I would mention it.

I was asked to provide a quote for a three day job in London (including 11pm finishes) starting tomorrow. Having factored in money for a hotel, I neglected to notice that the job was at Chelsea FC, and there is no such thing as cheap accommodation anywhere near Chelsea. Especially when booked last minute. Even the cheapest hotel was going to cost me most of the money that I had quoted for the entire job.

I phoned my sister who lives in north London, about 40 minutes from Chelsea, to ask if I could stay at hers. She said that I was welcome to stay, but she was going on holiday, so she would send me her keys in time for the following day.

September 10th

The keys to my sister's flat arrived first thing in the morning and Rachel dropped me at the station to board a train to the big smoke. In order to make my camera equipment more manageable to carry across London, I transferred it into a big rucksack with lenses and camera bodies wrapped in my boxer shorts and socks - very professional. I then had to squash in my laptop and enough clothes for three days. The bag was so heavy that I genuinely had trouble walking upright. I put it in the overhead baggage rack on the train and spent the entire journey worrying that it was going to fall off and crush the little old lady sitting next to me.

I arrived at Chelsea FC at 4pm, still with very little knowledge of what I was going to be photographing. I was hired by the events company, so the details of the actual event were all quite mysterious. I was hoping for something involving the Chelsea football squad, or at least Chelsea manager José Mourinho. It turned out to be a conference for the Human Resources department of an oil company. Hardly the rock 'n' roll job I was expecting.

The delegates all had a dinner, which was punctuated by speeches from various members of the board about how to improve various aspects of the company. Presumably they were all taking part in today's holiday - *Swap Ideas Day*. It eventually finished just after 11pm and I packed up my things ready to trek across London to my sister's flat.

'Did you check in at the hotel earlier, or have you got to do that now?' asked the events organiser.

'What hotel?'

'The hotel next door. We've booked you a room. Did you not get an email?'

'No, err, great. Thanks.'

'Where were you planning on sleeping?'

'North London,' I said sheepishly. 'But next door sounds much better.'

Needless to say the job instantly became a lot more appealing; a room in a nice hotel right next door, a buffet breakfast and no late night or early morning journey across London to contend with.

And then I found £50.*

*for those of you who haven't read *Every Day Is a Holiday*, this was a phrase, taught to me by my friend Ben, that you can tag on to the end of any boring story in order to try and inject excitement, and salvage some interest from it.

September 11th

Making your bed in the morning is apparently more important than you might think. Gretchen Rubin, the author of *The Happiness Project*, believes that outer order leads to inner calm, and the short time it takes to make a bed in the morning can have a dramatic effect on the rest of the day. Studies have also suggested that men who make their beds are more attractive to the opposite sex. I'm not very good at making our bed, which might help explain some marital issues. I do try occasionally, but my standards are so much slacker than Rachel's, and she always remakes any attempt of mine. I once stripped the bed, washed the sheets, duvet and pillow cases, and put them all back on without being asked. Rachel's comments on entering the room didn't do too much to persuade me to make this a regular thing.

'Have you done that deliberately just to annoy me?' she said.

'What do you mean?'

'The bedding. It's not ironed. Did you wash it and put it back un-ironed just annoy me?'

'Of course not. Why would I do that? I didn't know it had to be ironed.'

'Of course it does,' she said, stripping the bed again.

Since having children Rachel no longer irons bed linen either.

It was *Make Your Bed Day*. I was staying in a hotel, which is the one time when someone is actually paid to come and make your bed. Still, I was sure they'd be grateful for me helping them out, so before heading to the conference centre, I did my best to make the bed, which involved tucking in that annoying sheet thing that acts as a straightjacket, then doing the same with the irritating velvety hotel throw, before arranging a selection of about eight fancy pillows and thirty six scatter cushions into some sort of order. I have to confess that I did feel better leaving the room with a made bed. I was ready for the day. I had outer order and inner calm.

September 11th is always going to be remembered for one day that undoubtedly changed the world forever. It's a date that has so much significance that many of the other observance days that fall on September 11th are linked in some way to the terrorist attacks in America: *Remember Freedom Day, National Day of Service and Remembrance, Patriot Day, Libraries Remember Day.*

During the opening speech at the conference after breakfast, we had a minute's silence to remember those who lost their lives, and then they launched seamlessly into a presentation about graduate recruitment. The delegates all looked somewhat perplexed, and quite rightly found it hard to adjust back into corporate mode after such a sombre start to the morning.

The afternoon activities suddenly changed all of that, as the delegates were split into teams of six and unleashed on a three hour team-building exercise, which involved a sort of treasure hunt around London. They were each given travelcards for buses and the Underground, and they were required to find three different people at three different locations. After a day and a half listening to talks about 'blue sky scenarios' and 'thought showers', this sounded like the most exciting thing ever.

'I don't think you'll really be able to get any photos of this section of the day,' said the event organiser. 'You're probably best just waiting here for their return. There will be a chance to get some photos when they do the prize-giving later.'

'Oh,' I said dejectedly. 'Are you sure you don't want me to get some pictures when they are out and about? I'm happy to try.'

'Well you can try if you like. But we've had photographers before for this sort of thing and it's not very easy. They'll be racing all over the place.'

'Sounds like fun to me. I'm up for that.'

'Ok then. Go and speak to Pete and he'll sort you out with a travelcard, too.'

What followed were three of the most exhausting hours of my life. I looked around the room at the delegates beforehand and assumed I would be able to keep up with them, wherever they went. They were mostly overweight, middle-aged men in suits, or ladies in high heels and impractical business attire. They would be no match for me. I didn't realise they were all nipping back to their hotel rooms to change into trainers and more suitable clothing, and in some cases, lycra. They were taking this shit seriously. I was wearing my uncomfortable work shoes and a pair of impractical suit trousers. Equipped with a big SLR camera on each shoulder, and a heavy rucksack full of lenses on my back, I was at a slight disadvantage.

The groups raced off in different directions, some towards the nearest bus stop and others towards Fulham Broadway tube station. I latched onto one of the groups and gave chase, trying to take photos as I ran, whilst fumbling in my pocket for the travelcard, and navigating the turnstiles with a body laden with camera equipment.

I didn't want to just get photos of the same six people, so whenever we crossed paths with a different group, I tagged along with them instead. We visited the Albert Memorial, the Wellington Arch, the Natural History Museum, the Royal Albert Hall and many other locations, in the space of just a few hours. We rode countless buses, got several trains, ran, speed-walked and panted across London. I made it back to the conference room just in time for the 4pm deadline, as though I too would have had points deducted if I was late. I rushed into the room, wheezing and sweating, and randomly high-fived a couple of the delegates who seemed as excited as I was.

'Great job, guys. We did it!' I said.

'Yeah... er... well done you, too,' they said.

In the evening, we all went on the London Eye (my second visit of the year), but this time in darkness. London looks much better at night. As on Valentine's Day, I was on my own again with a group of people whom I didn't know, but thankfully this time there was no snogging or men preparing to propose.

They were then treated to dinner and a private after-hours tour of the London Film Museum, situated right next to the London Eye. The serious work personas of the delegates gradually faded throughout the course of the evening, as they became increasingly more and more drunk. A group of previously self-conscious people, who had been extremely reluctant to be photographed in the daytime, were now desperate for me to take photographs of them in compromising poses in the Film Museum, such as groping Darth Vadar manikins or pretending to suck off a yeti.

I returned to the hotel at 11:30pm and, despite my best efforts, my bed had been completely remade and the scatter cushions arranged in a different order. I personally think my way looked better, if I'm honest, but the chocolate on the pillow went some way to console it as I crawled into bed.

September 12th

I was into my third day at the hotel and was still unable to work the TV. It was a 'smart TV' and I could go on Facebook, Twitter and YouTube on it, but it was so smart that it didn't seem to function as a television. Today was *Video Games Day* so I spent ten minutes playing Angry Birds on the TV before breakfast, which, at 32 inches, was quite a surreal experience.

After the excitement of yesterday, I spent today photographing the delegates back in the conference room, listening to presentations about Human Resources and how to develop as a team. There are only a certain number of photos you can take of the same people sat around tables watching presentations.

As part of the job brief, I was asked to put together a selection of 200 photos onto a USB stick for the events company to turn into a slideshow for the grand finale of the conference. I have been a photographer for many years, but I had never sat and watched a group of people looking at my photos before. I usually put them onto a disc, or upload them to DropBox (other file-sharing websites are available) and send them to the client. It was a unique experience for me, and I felt a little uneasy. I knew I had done a pretty decent job of capturing the 'atmosphere' of the event, but there was not a huge amount of atmosphere to capture for most of it. I included plenty of fun pictures of the team-building exercise around London, scenic views from the London Eye, and I even threw in some of the drunken Darth Vadar and yeti photos.

As the slideshow started, set against a blaring, rousing soundtrack of M People's *Search for a Hero*, the tired and sleepy delegates started to show some emotion. Each photo was greeted with a laugh, an *'ahhhh'* or a shriek of embarrassment from the person pictured. I had only ever viewed my photos on a laptop screen. They looked awesome wall-sized.

As the slideshow closed with a shot of London by night, the delegates all started applauding, and then turned to look at me hiding away in the corner. I gave a self-conscious little wave and pretended to check some of my camera's settings.

I grabbed a couple of pastries from one of the tables on the way out, checked out of the hotel, and walked back to the train station to board a train back home, wishing that all photography jobs were as good as that. I realised what I had enjoyed most about the job was that it felt like I was working as part of a team for a change. Being self-employed is great, but it's a lonely business. Most of my interactions are done via email, and I don't often get the opportunity to work with familiar faces for any length of time. By the end of this three day job I felt like the event organisers, the audio-visual technicians, and many of the delegates, were work colleagues of mine.

I know this probably makes me come across as a sad loner. I'm not trying to evoke sympathy, as I chose to become self-employed. I just wanted to shed a little light on the loneliness of the self-employed photographer.

And then amazingly, I found another £50.

September 13th

Feeling exhausted after the last three days, I checked my diary hoping for a non-eventful day. I was disappointed to discover that September 13th is a particularly popular day of the year: *Blame Someone Else Day, International Chocolate Day, Kids Take Over the Kitchen Day, National Peanut Day* and *Roald Dahl Day*.

I managed to celebrate all of them in one go. I allowed the children to take over the kitchen. They mixed melted chocolate and peanuts together, and put them in fridge to make a chocolaty peanut thing, whilst I read a chapter of *George's Marvellous Medicine*. Rachel then came home from the supermarket, complained about the mess all over the floor, and I was able to blame someone else.

I checked my phone in the evening but the screen was blank. I tried turning it off and on again - the usual sure-fix for any electronic item - but nothing happened. I plugged it in but the green light showed that it was fully charged. At intervals throughout the evening I tried turning it on again, each time hoping that a brief rest would fix it. There was no sign of life. My phone was dead.

I am not particularly attached to my phone as a phone. I use it all of the time for checking emails and browsing the internet, but since moving to Devon all of the actual phone features have been completely useless, as I have no signal so cannot send or receive any calls and texts.

I have, however, become reliant on my phone for its camera. I use it all the time, and very, very rarely will I take my proper camera out for the day, as it is just too cumbersome.

I had not backed up the photos on my phone for over a year. I should have ticked the box that allowed for automatic backups on the 'cloud', but at the time I didn't like the idea of Google having access to everything. It felt like I was hard-wiring them to my brain. But now, with hundreds and hundreds of photos gone for good, ticking this box seemed like a sensible idea.

I also used my phone to take pictures for this book and the last one. I do email some of them to myself, send them to others, or upload them to Facebook, so some are recoverable, but many were only on that phone and were gone for good.

Friggatriskaidekaphobia is the fear of *Friday 13th*. The earliest written evidence of Friday 13th is in a biography of Gioachino Rossini by Henry Sutherland Edwards in 1869.

'if it be true that, like so many Italians, he regarded Fridays as an unlucky day and thirteen as an unlucky number, it is remarkable that on Friday 13th of November he passed away'

It is thought that the phobia of *Friday 13th* is an amalgamation of Friday, which was considered unlucky (there are references in the *Canterbury Tales*, and of course, Christians commemorate the crucifixion of Jesus on a Friday) and the number 13, which is considered unlucky because it follows the number 12 - a chronologically complete number (signs of the zodiac, months of the year, hours in a day/night, apostles of Jesus, years of the Buddhist cycle) - and 13 disrupts this completeness. There is also the connection with the Last Supper and having 13 people to dinner.

I had never been superstitious of *Friday 13th*. It is just another day. But my phone chose today to self-destruct for no apparent reason.

So fuck you, Friday the fucking 13th.

September 14th

The inconvenience of my phone being broken, and the thousands of lost photos, was soon forgotten with the celebration of *National Kreme Filled Donut Day*.

September 15th

Layla had only been at her new school for a couple of days when she received her first party invitation. Today was the day of the party and I drove her the two miles to her friend's house.

'Daddy, look it's Fred,' said Layla when we pulled up outside the house.

I looked down to see a kitten wandering about next to the car.

'Oh yes, it does look a little like Fred,' I said.

'No, Daddy. That IS Fred!' she said adamantly. I agreed that it did have a remarkable resemblance to Fred, but we were two miles from our house so it couldn't possibly be him. I did also think it was slightly unusual to see a kitten walking around on the road on his own.

'It doesn't just look like him. It IS him,' she said.

'But how did he get here?' I asked. 'Was he in the car with you?'

'No, I promise. I didn't see him at all.'

I phoned Rachel and asked her to check whether the kittens were both there. She called back a few minutes later to say she could only find Rocky. I concluded that Fred must have somehow climbed into the boot when I was putting the birthday present in, and then somehow sneaked out when I took the present out. I put Fred into the car and walked Layla to the party.

On the journey home, Fred kept climbing onto my lap and trying to lick at my face whilst I was driving. I had to gently push him through to the back seat, but the next thing I knew he was scrambling up my neck trying to hang on with his claws and then scratching his way up the side of my cheek. I screamed just as I drove past one of the mums who had been dropping her child off. The image of a screaming man, driving a car with a kitten attached to his face, must have been quite an alarming sight.

'How did you manage to take a kitten with you into town?' laughed Rachel.

'I didn't do it on purpose. I don't know how it got in the car.'

'Maybe Layla was hiding it.'

'No, I'm fairly sure she wasn't. She was more surprised than I was to see him.'

'You're not celebrating some silly holiday like *Take Your Pet to the Party Day* are you?'

'Ha, no. Although that is a great idea for a day. I'll have to register that one.'

September 16th

I stayed well away from Seattle today. I was all set for a visit but at the last minute realised it was *National Stay Away From Seattle Day*. The day is embraced by residents of the Pacific Northwest's *'Emerald City'* in a tongue-in-cheek way. They want to encourage tourists to stay away from their precious city.

Bizarrely, the day was created by a man from Pennsylvania named Thomas Roy, who confessed he had never even been to Seattle. Thomas Roy, as it turns out, is responsible for many of these strange holiday celebrations. He and his wife have registered approximately 80 of these 'special days'. So, thanks Thomas!

I can be quite an impulsive person when it comes to making decisions. I tend to go with my gut instinct and decide

113

on a plan of action fairly quickly. When it comes to spending money, I am the complete opposite. I very rarely (other than the Viagra I bought on *Viagra Day*) make an impulsive purchase. I am too tight. When buying anything of any significant size or cost - washing machine, fridge, camera - I'll research it to death on the internet, until I am completely sure I am getting the best value thing, for the cheapest possible price.

Today was different. Today I bought a surfboard on eBay. Just like that. Well I didn't just buy it from eBay. I WON it on eBay! That's why I love eBay (other online auctions are available. Are they? Probably). You don't just buy things, you WIN them. I love a good competition and the bidding process really brings out my competitive streak. You certainly don't get that in Aldi.

I searched for surfboards and sorted them by distance, and there happened to be one for sale a few miles from us. I don't know anything about surfing, or surfboards, but this one looked like it would do the job. The auction only had a couple of hours remaining so I returned just in time to steal the surfboard from under the nose of the highest bidder with only two seconds remaining. In your FACE, groovychick783! You might have a feedback score of 100% on 244 transactions but this surfboard is MINE! I did a Tim Henman style fist pump and ran into the kitchen to tell Rachel. She was surprisingly excited about my purchase, providing I let her use it, too.

I had promised myself that if we ever moved to Devon, I would buy a surfboard. I was adamant that I wanted to make the most of living near the sea, and for it to feel like a holiday for as long as possible.

My friend Damo was staying nearby for the week (his grandma apparently invented Banoffee Pie, don't you know?). He suggested that we hire surfboards one day while he was down, and this seemed like the incentive I needed to buy one.

It was also *Balance Awareness Week*, so surfing seemed as good a way as any to become aware of my balancing.

I drove to pick up the board from a balding, mildly overweight man in his early forties. He reminded me of me in a few years time, when I will probably realise that buying a surfboard was a silly idea. Still, for the moment I was a surfer. Or, at least, a man with a surfboard.

September 17th

I was sitting in the kitchen eating toast and drinking a cup of tea when Rachel came home early from the school run.

'Oh, how come you're back so early? I thought you were going straight on to mums and tots?' I asked, hastily trying to look like I had been busy, rather than just eating toast.

'I was. But we had another little hitch-hiker in the car again,' she said, holding up Fred the kitten.

'Really? He climbed in the car again? How did you not notice?'

'No. He wasn't inside the car. He was somewhere underneath the car.'

'What do you mean underneath the car? How?'

'I don't know, but I hadn't even got out the car at school and then I saw a lady in the rear-view mirror holding him. He must have climbed underneath the car somewhere.'

'Oh god, that's horrible. How did he hang on all the way there? That does make sense though. I didn't think I could have not noticed him climbing in and out of the car the other day. What are we going to do?'

'I don't know. I guess we'll just have to check underneath the car before we drive anywhere.'

'Good job we were only going short distances. Imagine if I had been driving back to Northampton? What a horrible thought.'

In the evening, we all got into the car as we had promised to take the kids crab fishing. Once everyone was in, I got down on my hands and knees and did a thorough search of the underside of the car, whistling and calling for Fred. There was no sign of him so I gave Rachel the all clear and we drove the few miles where we parked up by the estuary.

'Phew, no sign of Fred this time,' I said, as I got the crab lines out of the boot.

'Yes, there he is,' said Leo. 'I just saw his tail.'

I peered around the car but there was no sign of him.

'I don't think he came with us this time, pal. He must be back at the farm.'

'I did see him. I did. Look!' he said, pointing around the other side of the car where Fred was sat on the floor happily licking his paws.

'This is ridiculous. What are we going to do? You checked under the car as well this time,' said Rachel.

'He must be going right up into the engine where it's nice and warm. It's not going to end well if this carries on.'

'That makes me feel sick to think about it.'

'I'll take him back now. You all go and make a start with the crab fishing.'

September 18th

It was raining slightly, but not too cold, and the prospect of going surfing straight from the school run was slightly surreal. It felt a little different to the Northampton school routine of calling into the newsagent to pick up Doug's paper on the way home.

You can rent surfboards from a man at the beach, so I arranged to meet my friend Damo there so he could get kitted out.

'What the hell is that? Since when have you had a surfboard?' he said, as I got out of the car.

'Since the other day. Bought it on eBay. What do you think?'

'Not bad. How come you bought one?'

'I thought it would be a good idea. It might make me go more often.'

'And you have a wetsuit too?'

'I bought this a few years ago. Half price in Aldi. It's far too big for me but at least it makes it easier to put on.'

'Doesn't that mean it just fills up with water?'

'Yes, probably.'

We walked over to the surf rental van but there was no sign of the man.

'I think he's gone surfing,' said a surfer who was peeling off his wetsuit nearby.

'The man who rents the surfboards has gone out surfing? That's useful,' I said.

'Yeah, he's not the best businessman.'

'How's the surf?' I asked, trying to sound cool.

'It's pretty gnarly today.'

'Awesome,' I said, not knowing if this was a good or a bad thing.

I put on my wetsuit and started to rub the wax that Rachel had bought me on the underside of the board in a large circular motion like the diagram on the packet showed.

'You surfed before?' asked the surfer.

'Once. Several years ago, in Australia.'

'You do realise you are supposed to wax the top of the board, not the underneath?'

'Really? I thought it was to make it slide across the water better. That's what you do with a snowboard.'

'Snowboards slide across the snow. Surfboards just have to float on the water. The wax is to give your feet something to grip on to,' he said, trying not to laugh.

'Oh, Right. I see.'

I tied the leash to my ankle and tripped over it several times whilst walking across the already crowded beach, carrying my surfboard. Besides waxing the correct side of the board, and wearing a wetsuit that fits, the third rule of surfing seems to be to tie your leash onto your ankle once you get to the sea, NOT in the car park beforehand.

'You're a natural at this,' laughed Damo.

'You can talk. At least I've got a board and a wetsuit. You haven't got anything. You're the world's worst surfer.'

We looked out to sea and there were several surfers, but we had no idea which one was the rental guy, as they all looked the same. We tried shouting but they were too far out and the wind and waves were far too gnarly. Half an hour passed and he still hadn't returned, so I decided to brave it on my own. I spent the next twenty minutes getting thrown around by the waves, sliding on and off the board, and only once managing to get to my feet, but unfortunately on that occasion the wave had long gone. Damo was still without a board so I offered to let him do a shift with mine.

'Thanks. But I haven't got a wetsuit.'

'Borrow mine. It's one-size fits all.'

'No thanks. I bet you've done a piss in yours.'

'No I haven't! Well, maybe just a little. I warmed it up for you. You sure you don't want it?'

'Sure.'

The wax I had rubbed onto my surfboard had turned it into a giant lollipop, and every time I tried to jump on it, I slid right off the other side like a baby seal. I later found out you are supposed to use a special comb to etch grooves into the wax to allow grip, or rub sand into it to make it coarser.

Despite not actually doing any surfing, I enjoyed the whole thing immensely.

We celebrated *National Cheeseburger Day* with a cheeseburger from the food van in the car park. There was still no sign of the surfboard man by the time we left.

September 19th

'Is this tea mine?' asked Rachel as we were sorting out the kids' breakfast.

'It is, me hearties. Arrrrhhhh.'

'Why are you talking like that?'

'It's *International Talk Like a Pirate Day*.'

'Oh joy. I thought you'd done that one earlier in the year?'

'No. That was *Talk Like a Grizzled Prospector Day*. Arrrrrhhh'

'Of course. And they talk differently to pirates, do they?'

'Very. Arrhhhhh'.

'Does talking like a pirate just mean that you say Arrrhhh at the end of every sentence?'

'Pretty much, me hearties. Arrrhhhh.'

'I can see this getting a little annoying.'

'Hey kids. Today is *Talk Like a Pirate Day* so you can talk like a pirate all day.'

'Cool. Arrrrhhhhh,' shouted Layla.

'Arhhhhh,' growled Leo.

'Arrrhhhh,' repeated Kitty.

'Daddy, I've got a joke for you,' said Layla. 'Why are pirates called pirates?'

'I don't know. Why are pirates called pirates?' I said, expecting some nonsensical punch line.

'Because they arrrhhhhh.'

'That's actually very good. I'll make a note of that one.'

'Mummy, me hearty, is it time to go to school yet?' said Layla.

'Nearly Layla, me hearty, let's go and brush your teeth first. Arrrrhhh,' said Rachel.

'That's the spirit. Arhhhhh,' I said.

Talk Like a Pirate Day is one of those weird quirky holidays that has actually taken off and struck a chord with the general public. The day has increased in popularity every year, always trending on Twitter, and getting media coverage across the world. Arhhhh.

The idea was conceived by two friends, John Baur and Mark Summers from Albany, Oregon, during a game of racquetball. They started trading insults in pirate jargon and decided to form the holiday. They chose September 19th because it was the date of one of their ex-wife's birthday. What is unclear is whether she was an ex-wife because he spoke like a pirate incessantly.

September 20th

Since moving to Devon, I had done very little in the way of exercise. In fact, I had done almost nothing. I felt and acted like I was on a permanent holiday, which was great for the soul, but not so beneficial for my body. I was drinking and eating too much and exercising too little. I had let myself go.

Back in Northampton, I used to play football at least once a week, walk Layla to school each day, and run and cycle regularly. It was enough to keep me fit. Since moving to Devon, all of those activities have stopped. I started picking Leo up from pre-school at lunchtime each day on my bike. The pre-school is only a mile from our house, but it is a ridiculously hilly mile. I struggle to reach the top of the hills on my own, but with Leo on the back it makes it twice as hard. To be fair, he is great at encouraging me and utters a *'go on, Daddy, you can do it'* or a *'nearly at the top. Well done, you've done it!'* which makes all the difference.

More importantly, though, I rediscovered my love of cycling. I was never a cyclist before my end-to-end trip, and unfortunately had done nothing since. I did use my bike regularly in Northampton, but only to nip into town and it was always on roads swarming with cars. I had completely forgotten the exhilarating feeling of whizzing down a country lane, or the feeling of accomplishment at reaching the top of a long uphill slog. This achievement was made even better when I had my own whooping one-man fan club inches away from my ear.

Just this simple two mile bike ride each day had re-energised me and I could feel the familiar burn in my thighs that proved I had done some exercise. I was still grossly unfit, though. Picking up Leo from pre-school was one thing, as that was a commitment, but going out to do some exercise for the sake of exercise was very different. I decided I need something to train for in order to give me an incentive to get fit.

I ran my first marathon in 2009 - The London Marathon. I hated every single bit of it. I hated the training, I hated the build up to the race, and I hated the race itself. Every sodding metre of it was painful. I probably didn't help matters by beginning the race in a completely inappropriate starting group.

I had applied for the marathon on four previous occasions and been rejected each year. I was told of a technique of putting down a time that was either ridiculously fast, or ridiculously slow. The theory being that the majority of people put down an estimated finishing time of between 4-5 hours. The marathon organisers obviously don't want everyone finishing at the same time, and so like to have a broad spectrum of abilities. I've no idea if this is true, but it seemed to make sense, so I put down a time of seven hours the year I got my place.

I thought nothing of it until I was standing in my designated starting box and realised I was surrounded by people who were either morbidly obese, close to 100, or wearing fancy dress. I wasn't particularly fit at the time, but I hoped to run quicker than the people I was standing with. For almost the entire race I was dodging in and out of people of all shapes and sizes dressed in the most ridiculous costumes. It was like I was part of some strange 80s computer game. At the six mile point I ran past a fireman, wearing his full kit, complete with boots, breathing apparatus and an oxygen tank. He was travelling at a little above walking pace, yet it had taken me six miles to reach him. It was at this point that it was confirmed for me I had probably started in the wrong group.

My dad ran the very first London Marathon, in 1981, in a very respectable time of 3h 45m, which is far quicker than I will ever run a marathon. Growing up, my sister and I never took this accomplishment seriously, though. He had a framed photo of him crossing the finish line, and, also in the photo, crossing the line at the same time as my dad, was a very, very old looking man. We used to mock my dad that he only ran the marathon a split-second quicker than an old man. What we didn't know then was just completing a marathon is an incredible feat in itself, but more importantly, some older men are superhumanly fit, as my dad went on to prove, by running the London Marathon, 25 years later, in an even quicker time.

Still, with this reminder of dad's finishing photo at the forefront of my mind, I turned the corner onto The Mall for the final few hundred metres. I looked to my left and I was running alongside an old man. There was no way that I was going to be captured in the same photo as him, so I kicked hard (not at the old man) and managed to push ahead of him. I was running like my life depended on it, so that I knew he would be well out of shot. Then, just as I was approaching the finish line I looked to my right and discovered I was being overtaken by a man wearing a suit, complete with shirt and tie. This was even more humiliating than the old man, yet there was no time for me to get away from him. I was left with the only option but to hang back in order for him to get a few yards ahead of me and, again, out of shot. In my actual photo I am surrounded by proper looking runners. My children will never know that I was beaten by a man in a suit, as there is no photographic evidence. And it's not like I will divulge this secret in a book or anything.

Having hated every bit of the London Marathon, the moment I crossed the finish line it was all worthwhile, and I was already thinking about which one to do next.

I ran the Berlin Marathon the following year. It rained the entire time, and because the course is so flat, it was basically a 26-mile puddle. I then ran Chester in 2011 (just because my University friend lived there), and finally Milton Keynes in 2012 which put me off marathons completely, and running altogether. I hated visiting Milton Keynes at the best of times; walking around the shopping centre, especially at Christmas, was my idea of hell. It used to bring me out in cold sweats, and the only way to make Milton Keynes even more unpleasant was to run 26 miles around it in the rain.

After my first marathon, I made a vague pact with myself to run a marathon a year until I die. I don't plan to die whilst running a marathon; I meant that you can't really enter a marathon when you're dead - there is usually a clause in the terms and conditions. After Milton Keynes, though, I had no desire to continue this challenge so did not consider entering another. Now though, feeling restless in Devon, and getting more and more unfit and increasingly 'biggishly built', I knew that if the year disappeared and I hadn't run a marathon, I would be deeply disappointed in myself. The month of September is *Self Improvement Month* and *Healthy Aging Month*. There was only one thing for it. It was time for me to enter another marathon.

I Googled marathons in the UK, and there were very few scheduled for October, November, December (presumably because the weather conditions are so unreliable). But I did find one that looked hopeful - The Cornish Marathon. It was a relatively new marathon, which some call *'the toughest marathon in the UK'*, but I ignored this minor detail, because my eyes were drawn to something further down the page.

'A nice warm hoodie, medal, hot pasty and goody bag to all finishers'

A hoodie? AND a pasty? AND a goody bag? All for £20. This was a no-brainer. I filled in the form and my marathon challenge was back on. Just the small matter now of trying to get fit for it.

September 21st

It was our first completely free weekend in our new house; no visitors, no journeys back Northampton, and no plans. With so

124

many options of what to do, it seemed logical to let the holidays decide for us.

International Eat an Apple Day decided our breakfast. We ate an apple, in case you didn't work that out. It was also *International Coastal Cleanup Day*, so I suggested a walk on the beach to the kids and they were delighted by the idea. When I mentioned that we would be collecting rubbish they were less enthusiastic, until I cleverly rebranded it as a treasure hunt, and a competition to see who can find the most 'treasure'.

We drove to our nearest beach and began our cleanup operation. The children took it so seriously, and were so keen to collect the most treasure, that their definition of treasure became more and more broad. Soon seaweed was considered treasure, then shells, and finally sand, until we had three overflowing carrier bags of beach matter.

'Well done, guys, although I think you might have taken 'coastal cleanup' a little too literally,' I said.

'What do you mean?' asked Layla.

'You appear to have cleaned up the coast. We now have three bags full of beach.'

They all laughed.

There is over 11,000 miles of coastline in Great Britain, and I think we do a pretty good job of keeping it clean. By 'we' I mean we as a country, I'm not going to claim to be responsible for the entire British coastline. I remember holidays as a child and the beaches were a lot dirtier than they are today. This improvement is, I assume, down to a combination of stricter laws, increased awareness, and more effective clean up operations. Long may it continue.

'What date is it today?' asked Layla, back in the car.

'21st September,' I said.

'Saturday 21st?'

'Yes, why?'

'It's *Nickelodeon's Worldwide Day of Play* today. We have to go out and play somewhere and not watch TV.'

'Really? Are you sure? Where did you hear about that?'

'I saw it on TV,' she said, not getting the irony.

'She's right,' said Rachel, checking on her phone. '*Nickelodeon's Worldwide Day of Play* is on 21st September. *'We're dedicating an entire day towards getting outside and getting active!'* she said, in an American accent only slightly better than mine.

It was a nice idea from a TV channel, recognising the fact that television is not the only means of entertainment. They also stated that they would go off air for three hours during the day, which seemed like a noble gesture too.

'Well, I think we've already done that,' I argued. 'We were outside, we were getting active. We can tick that one of the list. Thanks, Layla.'

'But that wasn't playing,' she moaned. 'We were collecting rubbish.'

'Yeah, that wasn't playing. That was boring working,' added Leo.

'Boring? I thought you were having fun?'

'Not fun fun. Proper fun is not like that.'

'Ok, fair enough,' I said, pausing theatrically with my fingers on my chin. 'How about we get in the car and go to Woodlands.'

'YES!' shouted Layla and Leo in unison.

'YES!' shouted Kitty, who was not really paying attention, and seemed to be eating a huge handful of seaweed.

Woodlands Family Theme Park is, unsurprisingly, a theme park for all the family, set in some woodland. It's a very clever name. We had been there a couple of times over the years and the children all love it, and secretly, so do Rachel and I.

The day was a huge success and, at 4:30pm, with three totally worn out children, and two even more worn out grown-ups, we headed back to the car.

'That was the best day EVER. It was like being on holiday again,' said Layla.

On the way out I spotted a poster by the exit gate.

If you can't get enough of Woodlands, then why not sign up for our Annual Membership? Imagine a whole year of fun!

A WHOLE YEAR OF FUN? That was part of the concept behind my holiday project at the start, but it was clear that not all of the holidays were considered 'fun' by the whole family. In fact, the majority of them probably weren't fun for anyone. There was no doubt that we all had a fun day today, though, and it was amazing to see the excitement and energy in all three of the children.

'Maybe we should become annual members?' I whispered to Rachel.

'Really? It was a great day, but we don't want to come here every day.'

'You don't HAVE to come here every day. It would just give us the option to come more regularly. And if we were members then we could just call in for a couple of hours on some days, rather than feeling like we have to stay all day.'

'Sounds good to me, and I know the kids would love it.'

'Kids, how would you like it if we became members of Woodlands so that Every Day is a Holiday?'

'Wow, we can come here every day? Amazing!' shouted Leo.

'Well, no, sorry I didn't mean that. I was just referencing my book. I mean that we can come here more often. Would you like that?'

Judging by the whoops and screams that followed, it's fair to say that it was warmly received, so we signed up for annual passes there and then.

Worldwide Day of Play was an almighty success.

September 22nd

My parents were coming to Devon for a few days and I had not bought them their birthday presents yet. Both had birthdays in the previous few weeks, and I told them their presents would follow.

'What about getting them annual passes for Woodlands?' joked Rachel.

'Actually, that's not a bad idea. They enjoyed it when they came with us last year, and I'm sure they would go again. Good idea. I think I'll do that.'

It was only possible to buy the annual passes in person, so I decided to drive over to get them in time for my parents' arrival.

'I don't mean to be annoying,' said Rachel, 'but it says here that it's *World Car Free Day* today.'

'Really? What does that mean?'

'I assume it means you are not allowed to use a car.'

'But I need to get Mum and Dad's presents before tomorrow.'

'Well, it's up to you. That's what holiday it is today.'

'Who are you? The Holiday Police?'

'I'm just saying. I am your Administrative Professional, remember? I'm supposed to be helping you with this project.'

'Oh yeah.'

'You could always cycle there. You did say how much you love cycling again.'

I looked at my Ordnance Survey Map, which I was now a little obsessed with, and the route to Woodlands looked feasible. There was a network of nice quiet back roads leading all the way there, and it didn't look more than 10 miles each way.

'Ok, fine. I'll cycle. It might take me a couple of hours, though. Do you mind if I go out for a while?'

'No, that's fine. Take your time,' she said, with a little too much enthusiasm.

I went to get my bike but found that the back tyre was completely flat again, and the puncture repair kit had gone missing in the move. I had no choice but to take The Falcon.

Although fairly familiar with the local town, Rachel and I were both still completely clueless about the area in which we now lived, as we had not yet had a chance to explore our surroundings. To get to Layla's school, Leo's pre-school, the town, the beach, the swimming pool, we drive out of our house and then turn left. We had never turned right. The 'scenic' route that I decided to take today involved turning right. I was entering the unknown.

The road wound its way peacefully through the valley before I rounded a corner and was presented with one of Devon's finest, most brutal hills, stretching upwards (as hills tend to do) for what seemed like miles. As I reached what I thought was the top, I turned the corner and the relentless hill continued. The Falcon's cogs and bits grinded at the strain; its already seized parts had seized further having been neglected for so long.

I eventually reached the top and collapsed onto the grass verge to soak in the views. The fields, unchanged in hundreds of years, lapped down the hillside, and the valley snaked its way to the river estuary visible in the distance. It was breathtakingly beautiful. This was where we lived. This was our home.

The ride took me a lot longer than I expected, but it was such fun, and so exhilarating to be out on the bike again. The route had looked innocent enough on the map, but I'm not great with maps and forgot to pay any attention to the contour lines. The road was ridiculously hilly the entire way, and each long and gruelling ascent was followed by a terrifying downhill on a bike whose brakes didn't work on flat ground. It was so enjoyable, though, that I gave the occasional uncontrollable whoop, or laugh, as I cruised around the country lanes. It seemed as though everyone else was celebrating *World Car Free Day*, too, as I didn't meet a single the whole way there.

I had to stop at every junction to look at the map. With the high-banked hedges, and lack of any significant landmarks, it was hard to get any sense of where I was. I also noticed that at many of the junctions, the signposts had been snapped off, rendering it even more difficult to work out my location. This is perhaps a ploy by Devonians to keep the tourists away.

It took me well over an hour and a half to get to Woodlands, and I arrived hot and sweaty and out of breath. I successfully got the passes for my parents, and it was a bonus when I was able to get the OAP discount rate, too.

'Where have you been?' asked Rachel, when I eventually got home. 'I was worried about you. You've been gone over four hours.'

'I know, sorry. You wouldn't believe the hills around here. Don't EVER turn right when you leave our house. Let's only go left from now on.'

September 24th

Only a matter of weeks after moving away from Northampton, the town became one of the most talked about towns in the world, for a very unlikely reason. A mysterious clown began appearing in various places around the town, and, in particular, the Abington area in which we used to live. The clown bared a resemblance to Pennywise from Stephen King's horror movie *IT*, and had been pictured, mostly at night, standing in various locations around Northampton.

It was first spotted on Friday 13th, and nobody knew its identity, or what their motives were. The story made the local press, and then the national media took up the story, and before long it was being talked about across the world. An Irish friend of mine, who now lives in Buenos Aires, heard the story reported over there, and sent me a message asking if it was anything to do with me. A couple of other people that had read my book, and knew I was from Northampton, sent me messages asking if I was the Northampton Clown.

'Is the Northampton Clown one of your latest projects?'
'Are you the clown? Part of your next book?'

Unfortunately it was nothing to do with me. It was a really fun idea, and by the look of the clown's 150,000 likes on Facebook in the space of a week, an incredibly popular one. It was strange to see so many mentions of Northampton in the press, though, and it did make me feel a tinge of sadness. Nothing exciting ever happened in Northampton in all the years that we lived there, and I was now nostalgic for the town because of a mystery clown.

Todays holiday celebration was Punctuation Day. Punctuation Day celebrate's, encourage's and promote's the correct use of punctuation. I am not a Grammar Nazi. but I do appreciate correct punct-uation and try to use it; whenever possible, But sometime's I slip up like every one else'. This book has been profread several time's but some erors and in-corect use's of punctuation might have slipped throo. If you do spot any mistake's then please do contact me and I will amend them write away.

September 25th

As I mentioned in *Every Day Is a Holiday*, we try to eat as a family most nights. It's the reason I became biggishly built; after eating an early dinner together, I would then have another full dinner later in the evening. All sitting down together sounds very nice and idyllic in principle, but it's not. It's hell. Almost every single mealtime is an ordeal. Someone will moan that they don't like the look of what is on their plate, there are always spilled drinks, food all over the floor, tears, tantrums and hunger strikes. And that's just Rachel and me. The only reason we put ourselves through it is to try and keep that essence alive; we cling on to the faint hope that one day mealtimes will be enjoyable.

Today was *Family Day - A Day to Eat Dinner With Your Kids*. As a special treat, we decided to go to a local pub for dinner. Things didn't get off to the best start with Leo managing to knock over TWO drinks before we had even placed our food order. After that, though, they were all surprisingly well behaved. They all ate their dinner, sat quietly at the table after they had finished, and did some colouring with crayons that the waitress provided. In the car park afterwards, as a dad tried to strap his screaming children into the car parked next to ours, I heard him say, as he pointed over to our car, 'why can't you be well behaved and lovely like those children?'

That was the first, and no doubt last, time something like that had ever happened.

All we need to do now is somehow get them to replicate that behaviour on a daily basis, and particularly at home, and maybe mealtimes will become bearable.

September 28th

I had been back in Northampton all weekend for two consecutive weddings (and secretly hoping for a sighting of the clown). On Thursday evening I read up on Johnny Appleseed (an American missionary who introduced apples to various American states) to celebrate *Johnny Appleseed Day*, and I learned about Shamu the Whale - the first orca born in captivity - to celebrate *Shamu The Whale Day*. Then on Friday, I had a very awkward hug with a vegetarian at the wedding to celebrate *Hug A Vegetarian Day*.

As I was back in Northampton, it was a happy coincidence that today was *National Good Neighbour Day*. Despite living 250 miles away, I still strangely consider Doug my neighbour. Commuting back to Northampton for work was not ideal, but it did give me a great opportunity to meet up with friends, as I did on Thursday night, and visit Doug, Chris, and Basil.

I called in to see them before today's wedding. I had not told Doug I was coming, just in case I ran out of time.

'Georgie Boy!' he said as he opened the door. 'What a lovely surprise. Come here, kiddo. Let me give you a big hug. Come on in.'

Doug was on great form and, after I chatted to Chris, he ushered me towards the back door.

'I've got something to show you. Go and poke your head around the side of the house,' he said.

I stepped out into his garden and walked around the side. There, propped against the wall, was a shiny new bicycle.

'What do you think?' asked Doug.

'It looks great. Whose is it?' I asked.

'It's mine. It's my new toy.'

'Really? How long have you been cycling for?'

'Well I used to cycle all the time as a kid, but I hadn't been on a bike for 30 years until I bought this a couple of weeks ago. I read your book about the bike ride and it inspired me to get cycling again.'

'That's amazing. What about your arthritis? Is it not difficult to ride?'

'It's a bit tricky getting on and off it, but once I'm on there's no stopping me. You should see me whizzing along on it. I'm pretty nippy, you know.'

'I bet you are! How often do you get to ride it?'

'Every single day. I head off at about 6pm each evening, and I go and do a lap of the park, feed the ducks, and then come back. I'm only gone about half an hour. I can't leave Chris for much longer than that.'

'I'm so pleased for you, Doug. That's so exciting. It must be great just to get out.'

'Oh, it is, kiddo. I feel a bit cooped up when I'm here all day, so it's great to get out for a bit. It's nice to have a bit of time to myself, too.'

'You look like you've lost weight since I last saw you.'

'I have. I had to go out and buy a new set of clothes. I've lost over a stone just from popping out on the bike every day. And I feel so much better for it.'

'That's amazing, Doug. You look great. Good for you.'

Today I photographed the wedding of a girl I went to school with. It was a lovely, vintage-themed, summer wedding, with a marquee in a cricket field. I was just about to leave,

134

soon after the first dance, when the dancefloor cleared and in walked five beautiful burlesque dancers. They performed a 15 minute dance routine to the wedding guests. As a photographer, my job is to document the day, but it was very difficult for me not to look like a dirty pervert whilst taking photos of scantily clad women. Coincidentally, it was *International Lace Day*, so not only was I taking photos to document the wedding, I was also providing valuable evidence for my holiday celebrations.

I was too tired to drive back to Devon after consecutive weddings, so stayed another night in Northampton, and planned to drive home early the next morning.

September 29th

I was in the car by 5am and back in Devon while the rest of the family were still having breakfast.

'Hello. What are you doing back so early?' said Rachel.

'I thought I'd get on the road early, so that I didn't miss out another day with you all,' I said.

'Yey. We're glad you're home,' she said.

'That's nice. Have you all missed me?'

'Yes, we have. Mummy doesn't know how to work Netflix,' said Leo.

'Oh right.'

'I'm sure that's not the only reason they've missed you,' said Rachel.

'Yeah, yeah, whatever.'

'How was your weekend? Did the weddings go ok?'

'Yes, fine thanks.'

'Is it any special holidays today?'

'It is *National Attend Your Grandchild's Birth Day.*'

'What? Seriously?'

'Apparently so.'

'What a stupid holiday.'

'I know. I'm not planning on attending my grandchild's birth for many more years. In fact, I don't think I ever want to attend. Thankfully it's also *National Coffee Day*. I could definitely do with a coffee. Would you like one?'

'Yes please. I've already boiled the kettle. Twice. But I haven't made one yet.'

'I'll make a quick cup and then I guess I should sort out Netflix.'

September 30th

The last day of September is *Blasphemy Day*. Individuals or groups are openly encouraged to express their criticism, or even contempt, of religion. The date was chosen to coincide with the anniversary of the day in 2005 when a Danish newspaper published satirical cartoons of the prophet Muhammad. Violent protests were stirred up across the world, embassies were burned, and at least 137 people were killed. Regardless of my religious views, I am not going to criticise the opinions or beliefs of others, especially not for the sake of a stupid holiday celebration.

OCTOBER

October 1st

My highlights of the first half of this holiday challenge were the food challenges. First, there was *Man vs. Can*, when I ate unidentified canned food every day for a month. Then there was *Man vs. Ham*, when I ate an entire leg of Iberian smoked ham, in various incarnations, over the course of a month. It gave me a daily focus of the holiday challenge; something to base the other events around, and a common thread to help tie it all together. It was also great fun, improved my culinary skills, and gave me an avenue for creativity. Both food challenges were based around holiday celebrations (*Canned Food Month*, and, somewhat tenuously, *National Pig Month*).

It was time for another food challenge.

It was what this half of the year had been missing. But first, I needed a theme.

I looked through the October's monthly celebrations and there were several possibilities:

National Vegetarian Month - yawn

National Popcorn Popping Month - I would struggle to find a month's worth of popcorn based recipes

Seafood Month - very appropriate as we lived near the sea, and I could also call it *Man vs. Clam*. But buying fresh fish every day would be a bit of an ordeal, and quite expensive

Sausage Month/Cookie Month - extremely tempting, although too easy, and I didn't want to be more biggishly built than I already was

Pizza Month - see above

I then noticed *American Cheese Month*. I decided to interpret this as a celebration of cheeses, from the point of view of

Americans, rather than a celebration of American cheese. Americans are the best in the world at a lot of things. Unfortunately, making cheese is not one of them. In fact, I would suggest that America is propping up the very bottom of the *World Cheese League*, if there was such a thing.

Cheese was a perfect challenge; it comes in so many varieties, can be added to any meal, can be a meal in itself, is readily available, and is bloody delicious.

Man vs. Cheese is a rubbish name for a food challenge, though. Can and Ham both sort of rhymed with Man. And then I had an idea.

Man vs. Edam (other cheeses are available).

I decided to start immediately.

It was *World Vegetarian Day*, so my first cheese meal had to be a non-meat one. The majority of cheeses actually contain rennet, which is enzymes from animals' stomachs - but most vegetarians choose to ignore this minor detail, because cheese is so good, and it doesn't look or taste very meaty. To keep things simple, I opted for the classic cheese and crackers with a glass of red wine.

As with my other food challenges, I posted the photo on Facebook and minutes later Natasha, the resident food critic, had chirped up:

'*Yes... it is a Classic... but I'm not sure this is the level of imagination we're looking for in this challenge George!*'

She then followed up this remark with: '*Obviously - super excited to see a new Man 'Vs' though!! Whoop Whoop!!*'

I replied: '*Thanks Natasha. I seem to remember a similar level of cynicism on Day 1 of Man vs. Can. By the end you were begging for more.*'

October 2nd

It was *Name Your Car Day* today. Our car is already named *The Big Purple Bloater*. It is not the most flattering of names, but it is sort of a purple colour and its registration contains the word BLOTE. So there.

Greek salad with feta cheese

October 4th

Lots of posts started to appear all over social media about *World Smile Day*. I had originally ignored this one on my list, assuming it was another day promoted by the American Dental Association to try and get people to have their teeth whitened. *World Smile Day*, however, does not have a hidden agenda. It is genuinely a day to encourage people to smile, and to make others smile.

Harvey Ball was an American commercial artist, credited with designing the first smiley. The concept was created in ten minutes to fulfil a brief for the insurance company State Mutual. They wanted a smiley face they could use on pin badges and posters, to encourage staff members to smile at work, in an attempt to improve morale. The design was an instant hit, and rapidly spread beyond the company. Harvey Ball did not patent the design, and made just $45 (about $320 in today's money). Despite the runaway success, he never regretted not making more money and, very wisely, once said that he could 'only eat one steak at a time, drive one car at a time.'

Harvey grew concerned about how over-commercialised the image had become, and of how it had lost sight of its original meaning. So he created *World Smile Day*; a day when people are encouraged to devote one day each year to smiles and to acts of kindness across the world. It's a great idea, in principle, but then I thought about it a little more. People should be encouraged to smile and do good deeds ONCE a year? Really? Is that all people need to do? Surely people should be encouraged to smile EVERY day and do random acts of kindness EVERY day, not just one day a year. Every day should be World Smile Day. Come on, Harvey :)

Edam medley
- Edam on a gherkin boat
- Edam on a bed of chorizo
- Edam with a sphere of beetroot
- Edam on a crispy potato base
- Edam 'au natural' served in its own wax

October 6th

Mad Hatter Day is celebrated on October 6th in honour of the character from *Alice in Wonderland*. Interestingly (or not) he is not referred to as the Mad Hatter by Lewis Carroll - simply The Hatter. The phrase *'mad as a hatter'* pre-dates *Alice in Wonderland*, and is thought to come from the fact that mercury was used by hat-makers in the curing of felt, and would have been inhaled by the hatter. Mercury poisoning causes blurred vision and disturbed speech, and these symptoms were often mistaken as signs of madness.

The Hatter character wears a hat which has a card or price tag with the words: *In this style 10/6'*. This gives the pre-decimal price of ten shillings and six pence. The Americans, who created *Mad Hatter Day*, took this to symbolise a date so celebrate *Mad Hatter Day* on October 6th, even though if Lewis Carroll had intended it to be a date, it would have been June 10th.

Anyway, *Mad Hatter Day* is a day to celebrate silliness. I celebrated by phoning my friend Ben as we had not spoken for a few months.

'We never did get to do that Microadventure we talked about doing in the summer,' I said.

'I know, I was well up for that,' said Ben.

Back in March we went to a night of talks in London about various adventures, during which, adventurer Alistair Humphreys championed the concept of the Microadventure (or #Microadventure, as they are referred to on social media). The idea is that adventures don't have to be expensive, well-planned, far away expeditions, and it is quite possible to have an adventure whilst still having a real job and a normal life. Although many people work from 9-5pm, that still leaves the 5pm-9am free to use however you like.

'It's been a busy few months,' I said. 'Do you think that's it for this year? Is it too cold to squeeze in a hashtag microadventure before the end of the year?'

'Hell no,' said Ben. 'I am well up for one if you are.'

'I definitely am. Where shall we go?'

Ben lives in east London and I live in Devon, a distance of nearly 250 miles and about five hours apart. It is not the most practical long-distance friendship to be able to meet up for a single night, but that wasn't going to stop us.

'How about we just meet somewhere halfway between London and Devon?' I suggested.

'I like it. Let me just fire up Google Earth (other mapping software is available),' he said. 'Did you like that? I'm starting to sound a bit like you.'

'Ha, I'm honoured.'

I switched on my laptop too, and opened Google Earth.

'Right, I reckon that looks about midway,' said Ben, presumably pointing his finger at his computer, although being at the other end of a telephone, I can't be sure.

'What can you see?' I asked.

'Ok, a couple of inches left of Salisbury there is a lake surrounded by loads of green stuff. I assume that's grass. Looks pretty good from above anyway. And according to the map it's exactly halfway between us.'

'Yep, I think I see the one. The Wylye Valley? Is that what you're looking at?'

'That's it. What do you reckon?'

'Looks great,' I said, zooming in for a closer look. 'There's a pub right next to it called The Rainbow on the Lake. We could meet there and maybe have a quick beer before heading off.'

'Sounds even better. When shall we do it? I'm free whenever. How about tomorrow?'

'Er... yeah... tomorrow sounds good. The weather forecast looks pretty shit, but it is October. I don't think we can hope for much.'

'Let's do this. Fucking wicked! Hashtag microadventure, baby!'

Goat's cheese and red onion tart

October 7th

Rachel's parents had bought me a bivvy bag for my birthday, but it sat in a drawer with the tags still on it. I had never been on a Microadventure, so didn't really know what to pack. I filled a small rucksack with a sleeping bag, sleeping mat, my bivvy bag, some spare clothes and a few other bits. Ben and I discussed food very vaguely, but agreed we would both bring a few things and cook them on a campfire. How hard could it possibly be?

After a random, but delicious cheesy lunch of mushrooms and stilton on toast, I set off for our microadventure.

Ben decided to get the train, so I met him and his bike at Salisbury train station at 4:30pm. It had taken me over 3.5 hours to get there, as I inadvertently went too far up the M5 before heading into Wiltshire.

It was absolutely pissing it down when I pulled into the car park at the train station, and the thought of camping out was particularly depressing. The sight of Ben's smiley face, as he wheeled his bike towards me in his soggy hi-vis raincoat, cheered me up immensely. I gave him a big hug.

'Porge! Great to see you, dude,' he said. 'It's been too long.'

'Great to see you too, matey. Sorry I'm late. I got a bit lost. I ended up coming via Glastonbury.'

'Glastonbury? That's a bit of a detour.'

'I drove past the turning to Mrs Rogers's campsite.'

'No way! Not THE Mrs Rogers?' he said.

'That's the one.'

'Oh my god. I still have nightmares about that.'

We had stayed at Mrs Rogers's campsite during our Land's End to John O'Groats trip and Ben had an unfortunate 'incident' when he stated he was going to 'roger Mrs Rogers', unaware that she was standing nearby.

'You didn't call in to see her did you?' he said.

'Noooo. I put my foot on the accelerator and kept my head down.'

'Phew.'

We followed the road back out of Salisbury the same way I had driven in, until we saw the turn off for the pub we had spotted on the map. We pulled into the empty car park; the rain had relented slightly, leaving a light mist in the air.

'So what's the plan?' I asked.

'I don't mind. A quick pint and then head off into the unknown before it gets too dark?'

'Sounds like a great idea.'

The pub was closed.

'Oh bollocks. There goes that plan,' I said.

'I suppose we'll have to forget the pub and just go and scout out a place to sleep then. It will be dark soon anyway.'

We wandered through some scrubland on the far side of the pub and could see the lake beyond the hedgerow. A small track led to a padlocked gate, guarded by very prominent signs stating access was only to members of the fishing club. We made eye-contact with a fisherman who we could see across the car park. We held his gaze for a moment, debating ignoring the sign, hopping the gate, and looking for a place to sleep, but the fisherman was victorious. The thought of being woken first thing in the morning by an angry angler, holding a bag of hooks in one hand, and waving a priest in the other, was too daunting. A priest is a tool used for killing fish, by the way. He wouldn't be waving a man of the cloth above his head. Although that would have been even more unnerving, to be honest. The name priest was given to the fish killing tool because it, supposedly, administers the last rites to the fish. This seems a little unconvincing, but anyway I digress...

We trudged back up the track, past the pub, and into the village a little further down the road. We then followed the road through the village, and out the other side, over a river, and past some woodland.

To our left was the entrance to a nature reserve. The office was closed, but the gate was open, and, as Ben quite rightly pointed out, *'nature never closes'*.

The rain had stopped; there was not a breath of wind in the air, not another person to be seen, so we set off for a stroll around the reserve.

We soon reached the lake and could see the pub in the distance over the trees on the other side. There was a small, flat area by the water's edge, which looked ideal for us to sleep.

'I'd happily sleep here,' said Ben.

'Me too. It is very close to the main path, though. Any early morning dog walkers would see us.'

'Do you think that will be a problem? What are you worried they will do?'

'I'm not worried that they will do anything. It's just that we are probably not allowed to camp out here, so it would be best if we were somewhere we can't be seen, and then we'll have packed up and left in the morning without anyone ever knowing we were here.'

'Ok, fair enough,' he said. 'You brown nose.'

The main path diverted through the woods away from the lake, but a little further along we spotted a smaller path leading through the woods towards the lake again. We followed it to another level area at the water's edge. It was almost identical to the previous spot, but this time completely out of sight from the main path.

'This is bloody perfect,' said Ben.

'It's a pretty amazing spot, considering you found it on a map.'

It was genuinely beautiful. Ben had picked the location simply by pointing to Google Earth, at a place that was equidistant from each of our houses, and it just so happened that it was a really stunning spot.

The sun was beginning to set; there wasn't a ripple on the lake and, other than the roof of the pub in the distance, we could see no other sign of civilisation in any direction. Fishing was forbidden in this part of the lake, so we had no evil fishermen or priests to contend with either.

'Right. Shall we get a fire going? I'm getting hungry,' said Ben.

'Me too. What did you bring?'

'A tin of beans and some crisps. What about you?'

'Beans, too. Did you bring a pan to cook them in?'

'No. I thought you were bringing that?'

'I assumed you were.'

'Oh well. I'm sure we'll be able to just heat them up in their cans. It can't be that hard.'

'Shall we go back to the pub for a quick pint first?' I suggested. 'It will probably be open now.'

'Sounds like a brilliant idea.'

We gathered our belongings together. Thankfully we hadn't got as far as unpacking anything, so this just involved putting our rucksacks on our backs and retracing our steps to the pub. We made a mental note of where the path to our secret spot was, so we could locate it in the dark later.

Considering it was the middle of October, it was a surprisingly mild evening, but the warmth of the pub was a welcome relief. The place had a lovely cosy feel to it, with candles lining the bar and the tables. We ordered two pints, several packets of crisps and pork scratchings, and sat on a couple of comfy sofas in the corner. We were the only customers in the entire pub, but it had only been open for a few minutes.

'This is the life. What a great idea this was. Cheers Porge,' said Ben, raising his beer towards mine.

'Cheers,' I said. 'This is amazing. It's very tempting to sit here all evening and have dinner here.'

'I'm game if you are,' said Ben, leaning forward eagerly.

'It's not really in the spirit of a microadventure, though, is it?' I laughed.

'Fuck the microadventure. We've got two tins of beans and no means to cook them. We are using our initiative and survival skills by seeking food at the local pub.'

'You're so right,' I said. 'Fuck the microadventure! Let's eat here. I bet it's what Bear Grylls would do.'

'Awesome,' said Ben, reaching for a menu. 'I bloody love microadventures.'

Four pints later, a delicious meal of Toulouse sausages and mash, followed by Bread and Butter pudding, with salted caramel ice cream, we realised we were delaying the inevitable. It was time for us to head back out into the night.

As we settled our tab at the bar, the smiling, attractive bar lady asked us whether we were locals.

'No, I live in London and Georgie Boy lives in Devon,' said Ben.

'So what are you doing out here? Are you both on holiday?'

'No. We decided we hadn't met up for a while so looked at Google maps and pointed to this place, which exactly halfway between the two of us.'

'What a brilliant idea! Where are you staying? You're not driving are you?' she asked, looking at the empty pint glasses we had brought back to the bar.

'No, no don't worry. We're not driving anywhere,' I said.

'We're camping,' added Ben.

'Camping? In October?'

'Yes,' said Ben. 'Although we haven't even got a tent. Just a couple of sleeping bags really.'

'You're joking.'

'No. It's not too cold.'

'You're completely mad,' she said.

I am fairly sure that if we had asked, she would have let us sleep on the pub floor, but where was the fun in that? It was a lovely clear night, and I was looking forward to a night under the stars.

We made our way back in the dark to the spot we had scouted earlier. It looked even more beautiful at night.

'Look at the stars tonight. They're incredible,' I said.

'You don't get skies like that in London,' said Ben.

We decided to get our beds set up and try to light a fire, just so that we could feel like true adventurers.

'It better not rain tonight,' I said. 'The forecast is for heavy rain in the middle of the night.'

'It'll be ok. We can just zip up our bivvy bags if it does.'

'What do you mean?'

'Zip them up. So that the rain doesn't get in, of course.'

'Mine doesn't have a zip.'

'Of course it does. How else would you keep dry?'

'I don't think I do. Mine has a hood with a drawstring, but that's it,' I said, holding the top of my bivvy bag and letting the rest of it unroll to the floor.

'Ha ha, is that really your bivvy bag? Does it not even have a hoop?'

'What's a hoop?'

'A sort of curved pole that goes into the bivvy bag to hold it up, and keep it away from your face.'

'You mean like a tent?'

'No. Mine is a hooped bivvy bag.'

'Yours sounds like a tent to me.'

'Well it's not. That's what all bivvy bags are like these days. And I've got some guy ropes to stop me blowing about in the night if I wanted. But of course, I don't agree with guy ropes. Does yours have guy ropes?'

'Guy ropes? Are you serious? Does mine look like it has guy ropes? It's basically just a big bin liner.'

Ben unrolled his bag/tent and I was incredibly envious. He had the option of being left completely open at the top to get the full outdoor experience like me, or a layer of mesh could be zipped across to provide protection from insects, yet still be able to enjoy the fresh air, or it could be sealed completely shut, cocooning him in a warm waterproof chrysalis.

'Let's make a fire,' said Ben.

'Ok, just to prove that we can?'

'Exactly. It will make us feel more manly.'

'I took this old newspaper from the pub to burn.'

'Cool. I nabbed this pile of beer mats.'

We gathered together any sticks and branches we could find. Being in a forest, it wasn't too difficult. All of them were completely sodden due to days of persistent rain, though.

We screwed up the newspaper, built a pyramid of torn beer mats, stacked twigs over it, lit the fire (I had brought a lighter, by the way. I'm not going to pretend we successfully rubbed two wet sticks together) and the newspaper burst into flames, as newspaper has a habit of doing when put in contact with fire. The sticks crackled slightly, then the newspaper soon burnt out and we frantically tried to bring the smouldering damp paper back to life. It was no use. We had several more attempts, but we failed to get the wood to catch. We had failed as men.

'Good job we ate at the pub,' said Ben. 'Imagine if we'd had to try and cook our beans on that.'

Full of delicious food and slightly drunk, we slid ungraciously into our bags and lay down on the ground next to the tranquil lake. Staring up into the enormous night sky, I felt incredibly happy, and so glad we had decided to do this simple, and somewhat pointless, microadventure in the middle of Wiltshire.

'Night, mate,' I said to Ben. 'Thanks for coming. I'm glad we did this.'

'Me too. Thanks for suggesting it. It's been awesome. I hope you get some sleep in your plastic bag.'

'Thanks. I hope you get some sleep in your tent.'

'It's a bloody bivvy bag!'

'Yeah, whatever.'

I lay there for a few moments in the stillness, and drifted peacefully off to sleep.

I woke at 2am to raindrops the size of golf balls falling onto my face. I gasped and tried to roll over to shield some of the water from the opening in my bivvy bag. I couldn't move. I had foolishly opted to put my sleeping mat inside the bivvy bag to keep it dry, but this meant it was theoretically attached to me, and I was like an upturned turtle, frantically trying to right itself. Because the sleeping mat was inside my bag, it also meant that I could only pull the hood's drawstring to the width of the mat, which just so happened to be about the same width as the bivvy bag. So not only was my face exposed to the elements, but so was a two-foot long gap that I had no way of shielding. I pulled up the hood from my hoodie, and then used one of my arms to shield some of the rain that pummelled my face. I could feel the water streaming inside the bag and accumulating around my neck.

What followed were probably the longest two hours of my life. I thought the morning would never come. Despite how unpleasant it was, it did, in a clichéd sort of way, make me feel incredibly alive. The hood, arm and most of the upper part of my hoodie was completely sodden; my sleeping bag had absorbed all of the water that got into the bivvy bag and was soaked through.

I kept laughing to myself about the absurdity of the situation. I knew it was my own doing. I was sleeping in a plastic bag in England in October. What did I expect?

The rain eventually eased enough for me to sit up and retrieve my raincoat from the rucksack in which I had stashed it. I draped it over my head, and propped my arm up as a makeshift tent pole. I had, in effect, made a poor man's version of Ben's bivvy bag. I somehow managed to drift off to sleep again, and, when I awoke, the rain had stopped and the sun was rising.

October 8th

'You're alive!' said Ben.

'Oh. My. God. What a night!'

'I felt so sorry for you in all that rain, mate. I did call out to you a couple of times but I don't think you could hear me over the noise.'

'Oh well, I've never felt more excited to get out of bed, put it that way.'

'Have you got time for us to get some breakfast before you head home?'

'Definitely. There's always time for breakfast.'

We packed our bags and I gathered up the partially burnt, damp remains of the newspaper into a bin bag to dispose of. We had arrived at the nature reserve long after everyone had gone home, and left in the morning at 7am, long before anyone else arrived. We left no trace we had even been there. It was an extremely satisfying feeling.

We got a few odd looks as we walked through the quiet village, with armfuls of soggy possessions, back to the pub where we had left my car. We then called into a different pub on the way back to Salisbury for a very tasty full English breakfast.

'Did you carry on with that holiday project you were doing?' asked Ben over breakfast.

'Yes, I stuck at it. I'm just in the process of writing up the first half of the year and I decided to carry on and do the rest of the year, too.'

'Cool. So are you still celebrating them now?'

'Yes. In fact it was *Mad Hatter's Day* on Sunday which made me call you.'

'Oh, right, thanks. I'll take that as a compliment.'

'It was also *Country Inn Bed and Breakfast Day* yesterday, but somehow we celebrated that one by sleeping out in the rain.'

'Ha, that sounds far more civilised. Nowhere near as fun as our hashtag microadventure though. What about today?'

'Today is... err... *You Matter to Me Day*.'

'Aww, that's sweet, mate. And you decided to spend it with me?'

'Of course! Who else? Actually, I only found out it was *You Matter to Me Day* a few minutes ago when I checked my diary in the car.'

Our microadventure had been brief, but a huge success. We didn't take part in any activity, other than a couple of brief walks around a nature reserve, but it was a great excuse to catch up with a good friend, that would not otherwise have happened. That two hour section of the night was undoubtedly horrendous, but it was all self-inflicted so I had little cause for complaint.

During the three hour drive back to Devon I felt incredibly invigorated. My senses had been awakened, and I genuinely felt that the world looked a little different in my adventure-refreshed eyes.

The benefit of such an uncomfortable night is that normal luxuries, that we take for granted, are instantly revealed to mean more. When I got home, I had the best cup of tea I have ever tasted, the best hug from my wife (I told her how much she mattered to me), the nicest, warmest bath I have ever had, and that night my bed was softer and more comfortable than it had ever been before. Sometimes it takes a night of discomfort to make you appreciate how lucky you are.

I lived on the same corridor at university as a lovely girl named Heather. She was half-Polish (I think) and was particularly keen to show off Polish cuisine by regularly cooking strange Polish dishes for the rest of the corridor to eat. They all looked identical; always a beige/yellow colour, nearly always slimy, and usually containing cabbage. The rest of the people on the corridor didn't even pretend to like the food, and just politely refused to eat it. I had a reputation of having a big appetite, and because I didn't have the heart to refuse the food, was always the person that ended up eating it all. Thankfully, most of it tasted a lot nicer than it looked.

She once cooked a batch of pierogi, which are a form of Polish dumplings stuffed with various fillings including potato, cheese or meat. I made the mistake of saying that I liked them, and so she cooked another batch, and then another, and then another. I genuinely ate nothing else for a week. By the second day I felt like I had eaten my life's quota of pierogi, and by the end of the week I had developed a phobia of ever seeing another pierogi in my life.

Rachel recently read about pierogi in a book she was reading, and said she thought they sounded nice. I told her about my pierogi trauma and that I wasn't yet ready to eat another pierogi again.

Today was *Pierogi Day*. It was also *National Face Your Fears Day*, so I was given no choice.

Rachel kindly offered to cook them, and despite my insistence that she make a small batch, cooked enough to feed the entire town. I had rekindled my relationship with the pierogi, and was pleased to have sampled them again. The rest of the family admitted they weren't too keen, which means I will be eating nothing but pierogi for another week.

Cheese pierogi

October 9th

'Right, teeth time!' I shouted. 'It's time to go to school.'

'No it's not. It's not even 8 o'clock yet,' said Layla. 'We don't leave here until after 8.30am.'

'We are leaving earlier today,' I said.

'Why?'

'Because me, you, and Leo are walking instead of taking the car.'

'Ha ha. Very funny.'

'It's not a joke.'

'Why are we walking to school?'

'Because today is *Walk To School Day*.'

'No it isn't.'

'It is. Look at this. See!' I said, showing her my diary.

'What does that mean?'

'It means we have to walk to school.'

'But you just made up that day.'

'No I didn't. I didn't make up any of these days. They are all real days that other people decided have to be celebrated on these specific dates.'

'Who decided that we have to walk to school?'

'Well, according to Hoyle we need to walk today.'

'Alright,' she said. 'Leo, we've got to brush our teeth now.'

'Good girl. We don't want to be late for Shake 'n' Bake.'

'It's Wake and Shake, Daddy.'

'That's what I said, Shake 'n' Bake.'

'WAKE AND SHAKE! Why do you always say that to irritate me?'

Wake and shake is an initiative set up by Layla's primary school giving children the option of turning up 10 minutes early and doing an organised physical activity in the playground. It is basically just a ploy to try and ease the car congestion at school drop-off, but it's also a good idea to encourage children to be active, and get the blood circulating before the bell rings. I call it Shake 'n' Bake in reference to Will Ferrell's character's catchphrase in *Talladega Nights*. Layla doesn't get the reference but it annoys her so I keep it up.

School is only a mile from our house, but the road is very narrow and hilly, and it's not really suitable to walk along with a pushchair. So we always drive. It feels a bit wrong, but it's just not practical to walk with three children. But there is no reason - other than laziness - why I can't walk Layla and Leo to school, and leave Kitty at home with Rachel.

It was a rare sunny morning, the air was cool and refreshing, and it was nice to spend half an hour with just the two of them. Layla got to Shake 'n' Bake in plenty of time, and I ran home and repeated the process at the end of the day in reverse. I mean, I ran to school and walked back with Layla. I didn't run there backwards. That would be stupid.

It was really enjoyable, and considering the usual time spent finding a parking space on the school-run, it didn't take too much longer than driving.

'That was fun,' I said. 'Did you enjoy it?'

'It was ok, I suppose,' said Layla. 'Can we walk to school again tomorrow?'

Cheese and onion quiche with roast chilli potatoes and salad

October 10th

After a big bowl of porridge to celebrate *World Porridge Day*, I got in the car to drive back to Northampton for two back to back weddings at the weekend.

Perhaps by coincidence, or more likely through their planning, my parents were away for the weekend. It meant I had their house to myself, so I dropped off all of my stuff, and drove into town to visit Doug and Chris. Doug gave me his usual hug and welcomed me in.

'Are you still using your bike much?' I asked.

'As much as I can, kiddo. As much as I can. The weather has been a bit miserable recently and it's started to get darker in the evenings so I have to go at different times of the day, but I still try to get out.'

'That's great. And how are the knees?'

'Pretty good. I think the cycling helps. It keeps me moving so I don't seize up.'

The couple who had bought our house had moved in next door a few days previously. I peered over the wall into our old garden. It looked slightly sad and neglected. Not that it ever looked in great condition when we lived there, but it was always full of toys and bikes which at least made it appear lived in.

'How are you getting on with the neighbours?' I asked.

'Great. They are a lovely couple. Not as nice as you guys, of course, but they are both very nice.'

'That's good to hear. It must be more peaceful without having three children living there, though?'

'Oh, we miss the noise. We loved hearing the kids laughing and singing through the walls.'

'And the crying and screaming and shouting?' I said.

'Well, there wasn't too much of that. We do miss them.'

'They all miss you too,' I said. 'They are always asking after you.'

I walked up to the local corner shop to get Doug's paper like I used to. It was *International Newspaper Carrier Day* and I was perhaps celebrating it too literally, but it seemed to fit.

After spending a couple of hours at Doug's, I met some friends for a drink and a curry. When we lived in Northampton, we all met up maybe once every six months. This was the third time in five weeks that we had got together. I was seeing my Northampton friends far more than when we all lived within a mile of each other.

A curry is not the best meal to eat the night before a wedding, but I like to live dangerously,

Butter chicken with cheesy naan bread

October 12th

I drove home very late after the previous day's wedding, so that I was back home in plenty of time for my first Devon wedding; the wedding of our landlord's son. It was a step in the right direction, though. When we moved, my intention was to start building up wedding bookings down in Devon. The first booking fell into my lap so easily that I had done very little (nothing) in the way of marketing, so as well as being my first Devon booking, it was also my only one.

It was a welcome relief to drive one mile to the local church, rather than the 500 miles roundtrip back to Northampton, that I had been doing regularly. It was also a refreshing change to photograph a reception that overlooked the sea. I could get used to Devon wedding photography.

Today was *National Family Bowling Day*. Because I was working and because there are no bowling alleys anywhere near where we live, we all had a quick game of boules in the garden in the morning instead.

Up until recently, I used to be a kind, generous father, and ensure that I didn't completely humiliate my children with my amazing boules ability. Not anymore, though. Despite no apparent style or technique, and despite being six, Layla has an incredible talent at boules. I can't compete. I tried my hardest, but I was no match for her. The only way that I stood any chance was when it was my turn to throw the jack, and I could launch it to the other end of the garden, and beyond her physical capabilities.

Fish finger sandwich with cheese

October 14th

The Northampton Clown was unmasked today as a student from the town. A national newspaper photographed him entering a flat in normal clothes, flanked by two friends, before emerging in his clown attire. After several more appearances in recent weeks, the story gained momentum across the world. Despite huge support from many fans, he also claimed to have received over a thousand death-threats. It was fun while it lasted, but Northampton's month in the limelight was over.

National Kick Butt Day (not to be confused with *Kick BUTTS Day*, which is a designated day to help people quit smoking), is a day when you are encouraged to kick yourself in the butt, and give yourself encouragement to do those things you have been meaning to do. This holiday project has taught me to kick my own butt on a daily basis. Not literally, although I did just try it and spectacularly wiped-out on the kitchen floor. Each day, whether I like it or not, I have a holiday to observe, a diary to write, an experience to share, a butt to kick.

Earlier in the year, to celebrate *I'm Not Going to Take it Anymore*, I wrote a letter of complaint to an Archdeacon about the behaviour of a vicar in his parish. It didn't feel very honourable of me, but at the time I felt it was necessary. Today was *Clergy Appreciation Day*, so I wanted to balance out the negativity with some positive messages to vicars that I had met recently. I sent a few anonymous cards (I didn't want to appear like a complete weirdo) wishing them *Happy Clergy Appreciation Day*. If there is a god, hopefully he or she will allow this to cancel out my letter of complaint.

Cheese scones

October 16th

Thankfully there had been no further instances of Fred climbing into the car engine. However, it meant that we had to allow a few extra minutes for each journey, due to the pre-flight checks. Firstly, a thorough search of the underneath of the car on hands and knees; then the car bonnet had to be opened, and the spaces around the engine checked; finally, before setting off, we would sound the horn as a final deterrent. It seemed to be working.

It was getting increasingly cold (as tends to happen when the seasons change) and the wind and rain continued to batter our house on a daily basis. Although they are farm cats, Fred and Rocky are fed by Sally, and do have plenty of barns that they can sleep in, but for some reason they choose to sleep on our doorstep, so that we feel guilty each time we step over their shivering bodies.

Whenever we open the front door in bad weather, we find them huddled together on our doorstep. It is heartbreaking to see, but I have been very conscious not to feed them, or allow them into the house, as they are not our cats.

National Feral Cat Day changed all of that. I had no choice but to feed the feral cats. Anxious not to invite them into the house, I gave them a handful of cat biscuits on the doorstep. After what had happened with Doug and Father Dougal, I felt somewhat hypocritical, but these cats didn't have a home, so it did feel slightly different in my mind.

I felt the honourable thing would be to admit my weakness to Rachel.

'It's *National Feral Cat Day*, and I'm afraid I succumbed and gave a handful of cat biscuits to Fred and Rocky. Sorry.'

'Why are you sorry?'

'Because it's a bit hypocritical of me. They are not our cats and we said we wouldn't feed them.'

'Oh don't worry about it. I give them biscuits every time I go out there.'

'You do what?'

'Of course I do. They look so sad when they are shivering in a huddle on our doorstep. I can't resist.'

'If you're feeding them then that's why they are always on our doorstep.'

'I know. They are so cute though.'

Spaghetti bolognese with parmesan

October 17th

Half of the teachers in Layla's school went on strike. I understand that teachers need to make their point, and that striking certainly does that; but I also understand what an inconvenience it can be for parents, and that many people believe that teachers should be grateful to even have a job. I fall between the two camps, and I think a part of me still has the childish excitement of having a DAY OFF SCHOOL, even though I'm not the one that has to go to school.

Leo's pre-school is separate from the primary school and his teachers were not on strike. Leo is fairly reluctant to go to his pre-school on a good day, so when he discovered that Layla was not going to school he didn't take it too well.

'I'll miss you, Daddy,' he said, as I cycled up the ridiculously steep hill towards his pre-school.

'I'll miss you, too,' I panted.

'And I'll miss mummy and Layla and Kitty.'

'They will miss you too. But you'll be home again after lunch.'

He then went to hang his rucksack on his peg, and collect his name card to stick on the *'I am here'* board. His head was bowed and I could see he was in tears, but trying not to let me see. When he gets upset around Rachel he will sob quite openly, or hide behind a bush, or attach himself to a lamppost, and have to be forcefully removed, but for some reason with me he feels like he has to be extra brave. In a way this makes it even harder, because it is obvious that he is upset, but trying not to show it.

I gave him a hug, and one of the teachers sat him down at the jigsaw table.

I spent the morning editing wedding photos and trying to do a bit of writing, but Layla had other ideas. To her it was the weekend.

'Daddy, will you come on the trampoline with me? Shall we play Connect 4? Why are you working? It's not a school day.'

After lunch I admitted defeat. Rachel wasn't feeling very well, so I decided it would be best for all of us if I took Layla and Kitty with me to collect Leo from pre-school, and the four of us would go to Woodlands for the afternoon. It was *Wear Something Gaudy Day*, so I put on my fluorescent orange Oakley 20 hoodie.

The place was almost empty, and we spent most of the time playing in the Smugglers ball pool, which is normally reserved for older children. The kids delighted in me throwing them into the pool by their arms and legs, because it seemed like a clever way to bypass the *'no jumping'* rules that were plastered on the walls. I'm such a renegade maverick.

As we were getting ready to leave, the three of them teamed up together and shoved me into the ball pool. I made a theatrical dive - worthy of an Oscar - and threw myself into the middle of the pool. We all had a good laugh, until I checked the pockets of my shorts and realised that my car keys were missing. I looked back into the vast pool of balls and uttered a few choice words under my breath.

'Ok, guys, we are going to play a game called find the car keys. The object of the game is simple. You have to find the car keys.'

'Ok, give us a clue,' said Layla.

'They are in the ball pool,' I said.

'In the ball pool? You lost the car keys in the ball pool?'

'No, I didn't lose them. I have hidden them. That's the game.'

'No, you lost them and you want us to find them. You eejit.'

'I know exactly where they are. You just have to find them. And where did you get the word 'eejit' from?'

'It's what Mummy calls you.'

'Oh, does she now? Well the person who finds the keys gets 20p!'

'20p? For finding the keys you lost? Is that all?' shouted Layla.

'OK, fine. 50p. And I didn't lose them. I hid them.'

'Yeah right,' she said, and jumped into the pool.

Kitty and Leo jumped in after her and they all started frantically throwing the balls around trying to locate the keys. I watched them with a false grin, and offered words of encouragement, whilst secretly praying that I wouldn't have to phone Rachel to tell her we were all stranded at Woodlands because I had lost the car keys in a ball pool.

After a couple of minutes I joined them in the pool.

'But I thought you knew where they were, Daddy?' asked Layla.

'I do. I'm just pretending for Leo and Kitty.'

After a few minutes Leo emerged from the depths triumphantly clutching the car keys.

'Brilliant, well done, Leo,' I said, breathing a sigh of relief.

'Ooooh, that's not fair. Leo gets 50p and I don't,' said Layla.

'Well as a treat for helping, you can all have an ice-cream for pudding later. Let's go.'

'What's for dinner?' asked Leo in the car.

'Cheesy pasta! It's *National Pasta Day*, and *American Cheese Month*.'

'Yey, I love pasta.'

'How was Woodlands?' asked Rachel when we got home.
'Good thanks.'
'Daddy lost car keys in ball pool,' said Kitty.
'Did he? The eejit,' said Rachel.

Macaroni cheese

October 18th

One of the last things my grandma said to me before she died was that I looked like the former president of Iran, Mahmoud Ahmadinejad. I wasn't too offended by the comparison. He's a good looking man, and there are far worse former Middle Eastern leaders that I could have been compared to; Saddam Hussein, for example.

The main reason, actually pretty much the only reason, that she likened me to Mahmoud Ahmadinejad, was that I had a beard. My grandma hated beards. My cousins all have beards and she would regularly tell them that they looked like Tom Hanks in the film *Castaway*, or sometimes Jesus.

I very rarely shave. I have a beard trimmer that I use once a week at the most. It's for a combination of reasons; partly laziness, but also because I prefer having a bit of stubble and, also, because I shave so infrequently, when I do my neck goes all spotty like a teenage boy.

169

Today was *No Beard Day*. It was time to shave. Only I didn't have a razor or any shaving gel. I managed to locate a blunt razor Rachel uses to shave her legs, and some shower gel worked as makeshift shaving foam. It felt like I was a young boy going through puberty and shaving for the first time again; my face was all blotchy and covered in small cuts.

'Haha, you'll look good at the dinner party tonight,' laughed Rachel.

'What dinner party?'

'We're going to Jo and Scott's, remember?'

'Oh bollocks, I'd forgotten. Why did it have to be *No Beard Day* today? I look like a right bellend.'

Lunch: crispy herb-crusted bread batons, with a white cheese dipping sauce

The very thought of dinner parties terrifies me, especially ones at which I don't know any of the people, which was probably why I had blocked this one from my mind. I knew that it was important that we try and socialise and meet new people, and to be invited to someone's house was a real honour.

The evening was very enjoyable and nowhere near as scary as I had imagined. There was a 'celebrity' guest-of-honour, whom I unfortunately didn't recognise. Scott, whose house it was, is a TV cameraman and the 'celebrity' and I had a long chat about how they worked together, and I had assumed that he too was a cameraman. It later transpired that he was the presenter, and I had to do some quick backtracking. He was in the process of writing his memoirs and had hired a beach house for a few months while he wrote it. It sounded like a lovely romantic idea of writing a book; disappearing and shutting yourself away from the world, and all its distractions, whilst focusing on the task of writing a book. I'm not saying that I would want to spend a long period of time away from my family, but I am sure it would make the writing process a whole lot easier.

'Did you know George has written a book?' said Rachel to the 'celebrity'.

'No, what's it about?' he asked, mildly enthusiastically.

I was having a conversation with another guest at the time, but was also trying to eavesdrop on Rachel's conversation.

'It's about a bike ride that he did from Land's End to John O'Groats. You should talk to him about it.'

'Sounds fascinating. I will.'

Thankfully he didn't.

I hate talking to people about any of my books. When I wrote my first book I didn't mention it to anyone apart from Rachel, and she knew I didn't want to talk about it so never asked. I didn't want the added weight of expectation of people knowing I was trying to write a book. Firstly, I didn't even know if I would ever finish it, let alone publish it. Then there was the added pressure of being constantly asked 'how's the book coming along?' or 'have you got a publishing deal yet?' By not telling anyone, the only pressure I received was from me. If I had never finished it then nobody would ever have known - not that there is any shame in not completing a book. I also liked the idea of it being a surprise to people once completed.

I am also uncomfortable talking to people about my book even now that it is published. I am very happy to spend my time going on about it on social media, and to people whom I haven't met, but when it comes to talking to friends about it in person, I try and avoid it whenever possible.

October 19th

After breakfast we put the kids' bikes in the car and drove to a National Trust property nearby. Layla and Leo ride their bikes quite a lot, but they have never been on a bike ride with a start and a finish. I know that any bike ride technically has a start and a finish, but I mean a, well, a proper bike ride.

We followed a track that wound its way down through the woods and along the river. Kitty - who is still too young to ride a bike properly - fell asleep in the buggy and so Rachel and I jogged and walked quickly to try and keep up with the other two. It was amazing to watch them having such fun. Despite being two and a half years younger than Layla, Leo is the more competent cyclist. He's taken to cycling like a duck to water. Or, like a kid to cycling. He rode a balance bike from the age of two and we got him his first 'big bike' for his third birthday. The stabilisers came off after the second attempt (we took them off, they didn't just fall off). He still sees Layla as his big sister, though, and doesn't like to stray too far from her, or make her feel too slow, so they cycled alongside each other in rare harmony. Cycling really does calm people down.

It was *Evaluate Your Life Day*, and at that very moment, speed-walking along with Rachel, Kitty fast asleep in the buggy, and the other two riding along, side by side, I suddenly realised how lucky and how happy I was.

Mozzarella, tomato and basil

October 20th

My marathon training had not been going to plan. I had been on a couple of runs every week, but nothing more than six miles. The marathon was less than a month away, and I knew I would have to increase things, otherwise there would be no way I would be able to claim my much sought-after hoodie and pasty.

I decided to attempt my longest run for 18 months. I would run to the sea and back. I understand that a huge proportion of UK residents live a short distance from the sea, but having spent almost my entire life in Northampton, it is still an amazing concept to me. Northampton is one of the furthest points from the coast in the whole of the UK, and during the entire time I lived there, we had one day trip to the beach. We went to Hunstanton when Layla was a toddler, and Leo was only a few months old. It was low tide, in the middle of winter, and the sea was a distant glimmer on the horizon. We walked through sticky, wet, sandy mud for what seemed like miles, and gave up before we even got to the sea.

Things are different now we live in Devon; there are endless beaches within a short drive from us. But I had never run to the sea. I looked on my trusty Ordnance Survey map and plotted a mental route from our house. I mean that I plotted the route in my mind, not a lunatic route.

It was pretty much a straight line the entire way, along quiet back roads, and a short section along what appeared to be a bridleway, before meeting the road again for the last couple of miles down to the coast. I estimated it would be about a 13 mile roundtrip.

I had been fooled by the contour lines yet again, and the quiet country road turned out to be a set of ridiculous hills that continued for miles, and the bridleway was a terrifyingly steep, winding, rocky and slippery descent into a forest and then up the treacherous, muddy, brambly path on the other side of the valley. It was the sort of place that if I had slipped and broke a leg it would have been several weeks before I was found.

I eventually reached the sea, and despite it being late October, it was a bright, sunny day and I was desperate for a swim. I took off my trainers and t-shirt and ran straight in to the ball-numbingly freezing water.

The run home was as bad as the way there, with the added discomfort of a pair of soggy, salty wet shorts, which itched and chafed the entire way back. It was still an invigorating, and extremely rewarding experience, and I felt a lot better for it.

A mature cheddar and chutney tower, served with beechwood smoked ham and a scattering of Wheat Crunchies

It was *World Toy Camera Day*. I assumed that a 'toy' camera was just that - a toy. You look through the viewfinder, click the button and a funny picture of a kitten appears. You click the button again, and this time a puppy clutching a flower appears, and so on. But *World Toy Camera Day* celebrates simple plastic lens film cameras, or even disposable cameras. I mentioned in *Every Day Is a Holiday* what a lack of success my homemade pinhole camera had been, but I decided to try and convince the children that a disposable camera was still a wonderful thing. After some hunting around I found them for sale in a local newsagent and showed it to Layla, Leo and Kitty, and asked if they wanted to take some photos.

'Me first, me first!' shouted Leo.

'Ok, but just take two photos and then it's Layla's go,' I said.

'Oh, why can I only take TWO photos?'

'Because you can't take lots of photos with this camera. You can only take 24. It's a special camera.'

'24?' said Layla, 'That's not very many.'

They both took their two photos, carefully considering what they should take them of; Leo took one each of Fred and

175

Rocky, Layla took one of the kittens and one of me, and Kitty took both hers of her feet.

'Why can't I see our pictures on the camera?' asked Leo.

'Because this camera is different. You can't see them on the camera.'

'Will you show us them on the computer later?' asked Layla.

'No. Once we have taken all of the 24 pictures then we have to send the camera away for the film inside to get printed, or we can take it into a shop and wait for them to print them there.'

'And then can we take 24 more pictures?' asked Layla.

'No, then this camera won't work anymore so we will have to buy another one. But we probably won't,' I added, realising again how great digital photography is.

'So why are we playing with it today?'

'Because it's *World Toy Camera Day* today, so we are supposed to play with a toy camera.'

'But this isn't a toy. It's just a rubbish camera. What about my toy camera?'

'But yours doesn't take real photos. It just shows pictures of kittens and puppies with flowers.'

'My one takes real photos.'

'Does it?'

'Yes, look,' she said, thrusting a blue camera in my face.

"Oh yeah. I'd forgotten about this one. Does it still work?"

We had bought it for Layla for Christmas a few years ago, but it was a bit temperamental and kept breaking. I put some new batteries in it and to my surprise it actually worked. This was a proper toy camera.

'Let me take a photo of you and mummy,' she said, fiddling around with a few buttons before framing us and taking a photo.

176

She had used a template of a bride and groom in their wedding attire with our heads in the frame. We both laughed.

'You should use this as your camera at weddings, Daddy. Then people wouldn't have to put special clothes on,' she said.

'What a great idea. I think you might be on to something there.'

October 21st

My computer's Desktop makes me feel agitated whenever I look at it. Every file, download, or email attachment I receive I click *'save to Desktop'* so that I can find it instantly when I need it. That all worked fine in principle, until it got to the stage that my entire desktop was full of icons, and not only was it hard to see them, but most of them were not even visible as they were off the screen.

I had 259 files and folders saved on my desktop. Most of them I had no use for anymore and the rest of them were not important enough to warrant being right there in my face every time I turned on my computer. *Clean Your Virtual Desktop Day* was the incentive that I needed to finally clear off all that crap. I did something fairly similar in the first half of the year. In fact, it seems that a high-proportion of these holidays involve tidying or de-cluttering. I kept checking on the internet that they are actually real, and not just days written into my diary by Rachel to get me to do things.

I went through the files on my computer's desktop one by one, either deleting them or filing them somewhere more appropriate. The whole process took me two hours, but I felt so much better afterwards. All that was left on my desktop was the Recycle Bin, which I then satisfyingly emptied. There are not many better sounds than the noise that it makes when it's emptied. It was also *Information Overload Day* and *Celebration of the Mind Day*, and by cleaning my virtual desktop, I had celebrated both of these, too.

I agree, I definitely need to get out more.

Marmite pasta with ketchup and parmesan

OCTOBER 22ND

THE CAPS LOCK BUTTON GETS A LOT OF BAD PRESS. IT'S TRUE THAT PEOPLE DO OFTEN ABUSE IT AND IT CAN COME ACROSS AS QUITE RUDE AND AGGRESSIVE. I QUITE LIKE IT, THOUGH, AND I THINK THAT WHEN USED IN MODERATION IT CAN BE QUITE EFFECTIVE. OBVIOUSLY IT'S A BIT DIFFICULT TO GIVE YOU AN EXAMPLE WHEN I AM WRITING LIKE THIS. I AM NOT SHOUTING, BY THE WAY. I AM VERY CALM AND THIS SHOULD BE READ IN A SLOW, MILD MANNER.

TODAY IS *INTERNATIONAL CAPS LOCK DAY*. SOME PEOPLE USE THE DAY AS A MEANS TO CAMPAIGN FOR ITS ABOLITION, BELIEVEING THAT IT SERVES NO GOOD PURPOSE, AND CAUSES

PEOPLE TO USE IT TO SHOW ANGER. PEOPLE ALSO SUGGEST IT SHOULD BE ERADICATED BECAUSE IT IS EASILY PRESSED ACCIDENTALLY, AND THEN HUGE CHUNKS OF TEXT ARE TYPED IN CAPITALS BY MISTAKE. PERSONALLY, I THINK THAT IF PEOPLE AREN'T ABLE TO LOOK UP AT THEIR COMPUTER SCREEN EVERY FEW WORDS, THEN THEY PROBABLY SHOULDN'T BE USING A COMPUTER IN THE FIRST PLACE.

BAKED CAMENBERT, CHORIZO AND FRESHLY BAKED BREAD

oCTOBER 23RD

tHA'TS BETTER. i CAN RELAX NOW AFTER A DAY OF CAPS LOCKS. Oh bollocks, I too am one of those morons that leave it on accidentally.

I am getting confused about all the comings and goings of swallows and slugs from San Juan Capistrano. May 28th was *Slugs Return from* San *Juan Capistrano Day,* March 19th was *Swallows Return to San Juan Capistrano Day* and today was

179

Swallows Depart from San Juan Capistrano Day. When do the slugs go back? Who knows? More to the point - who gives a shit?

The swallows that nest in the barns by our house have all departed. They've set off on their 6000 mile journey to South Africa. It's a staggering feat, if you think about it. Swallows can travel up to 200 miles per day as they cross Europe, the Mediterranean, Morocco and then down through Africa, with a large proportion of them crossing the Sahara desert. Many of them die from starvation, exhaustion or during bad weather. Because of our cold winters and lack of food, I understand why they make this epic trip to South Africa. What I don't understand is why they bother returning. If I was a swallow I'd just stay in South Africa all year long.

National Mole Day was a bit of a disappointment. I thought it was a day to celebrate the little furry creature that buries underground, leaving mounds of earth on people's lawns, but it's actually about chemistry. The day is celebrated by chemists and chemistry students between 6:02am and 6:02pm on October 23rd. This makes the date and time (if you chose to write it down in this unusual, but convenient for their purposes, way), 6:02 10/23. The time and date are derived from Avogadro's constant, which is approximately 6.02×10^{23} and refers to the number of particles in one mole of substance. I'm not going to pretend I understand what the hell all this really means. Each year, *Mole Day* is given a different theme using a vague pun on the word 'mole'. In previous years the themes have been *'The Mole the Merrier'*, *'Rock 'n' Mole'*, *'Secret Agent Double Mole Seven in Moles are Forever'* and the year 2000 one - *'Celebrate the Molennium'*. This year the theme is *'Animole Kingdom'*.

I celebrated *Mole Day* with breakfast at McDonald's. I had a Sausage and Egg McMolefin (with cheese).

I'll get my coat.

October 25th

'Mummy, Daddy, come and see what we've done,' said Leo.

'What have you done?' I asked.

'Kitty and I have made a height chart.'

'A height chart? What do you mean?' asked Rachel, looking at me with a worried expression on her face.

'Like the one you did of all of us at our old house.'

Back in Northampton, we made a few light pencil marks of their heights on the door frame of the kitchen. If Leo had made his own, it was slightly concerning to imagine what it looked like.

We followed him into the next room and it took a fraction of a second to locate his height chart. There, in big letters, scrawled on the wall in felt tip pen, were the words '*Leo*' and '*Kitty*' written alongside a line that stretched from the floor to the ceiling.

In the spirit of today's holiday - *National Forgiveness Day* - we didn't get too cross, but we did have some stern words with him about how naughty it is to draw on the walls.

'But you and Mummy used to write on the walls at our old house,' he said.

'Yes, but that was only in pencil. It wasn't very noticeable and it rubbed off easily.'

'This rubs off too. Look!' he said, pulling up his sleeve and rubbing at the letters which started to smudge across the wall.

'Just leave it, Leo,' said Rachel. 'Don't worry, we know you weren't trying to be naughty. Don't write on the walls again though. Ok?'

'Ok.'

To his credit, his writing was very neat, but I did question the accuracy of his measuring. Kitty had apparently had a growth spurt and was now twice as big as Leo, who was only a couple of feet tall.

Sausages and spicy chips, with a watermelon and feta salad (it seemed like a good idea at the time)

In the evening I watched *Child's Play* to celebrate *Chucky the Notorious Killer Doll Day* and I went to bed a nervous wreck.

October 27th

We had all driven back to Northampton for the weekend, and while I photographed a wedding yesterday, Rachel and the kids visited lots of friends in and around Northampton. This morning we called over to see Rachel's granddad and then on to visit Doug and Chris.

As we pulled up outside, Rachel had a slight panic. It was the first time she had visited since the new people had moved into our old house.

'I don't think I can go in,' she said.

'Why not?'

'It just feels too weird,' she said. 'I don't want to look out into our old garden.'

'It's fine. I thought it would be weird, but it's really not. It looks different when it has other people's things in it anyway. It doesn't really look or feel like our old garden.'

'I know, that's what worries me.'

'What do you want to do then? Shall we just go in and you can go for a drive and come and pick us up in a bit?'

'No. I want to see Doug and Chris and Father Dougal. I just find it all a bit weird.'

'It'll be fine. I promise.'

Doug and Chris were both absolutely thrilled to see Rachel, Layla, Leo and Kitty. Although they like it when I visit, all they usually talk about is Rachel and the kids, so it was nice for them finally to be able to pay a visit. Doug took it in turns to give them rides up the stairs on his stair lift, and I was just gutted he didn't offer me a go.

Rachel soon forgot her concerns and chatted along as if we'd never moved away.

It was *Mother-In-Law Day* so we accepted an invitation to have lunch with Rachel's parents before driving back down to Devon. We would of course have accepted even if it had not been *Mother-In-Law Day*. We're not monsters.

Cheesecake

October 28th

The UK had been experiencing one of the wettest months since records began. The wind and rain had been relentless and our local town regularly flooded.

We drove back from Northampton last night, during what forecasters said was going to be the EYE OF THE STORM. Weather like never seen before was going to hit Great Britain and the south west was going to be particularly badly affected.

The rain was noticeably horrendous, and for the final 15 miles of our journey, we drove through a continuous three-inch deep puddle. Rachel sat in the passenger seat screaming each time we hit water, and, as the water was continuous, she screamed without pause for about half an hour. Rachel is not the calmest of passengers. I tend to do most of the driving (because I am an even worse passenger), but she will frequently fall asleep soon after the kids have, but whilst they sleep soundly for the duration, Rachel will then wake up at regular intervals on the motorway and panic that I am also asleep and veering into the central reservation. She will grab hold of my leg and shout to make sure I am awake. This then makes me panic, and often swerve towards the central reservation.

Despite the rain last night, the storm didn't seem as bad as had been predicted. There were a few small branches littering the road, but there was no real sign of any other destruction. We arrived back at our house, just after 1am, and the rain had subsided. We went to bed thinking that a lot of fuss had been made over nothing.

When we woke up this morning, I looked out of the kitchen window during breakfast. The sun was out, and the farmyard looked remarkably calm and tranquil. I could see the birds on the wall, and in the distance, a horse, nosing his head out of his stable. What? How could I see the other side of the farmyard so clearly? Normally my view was impeded by the netting of a 12 foot trampoline. Who had moved the trampoline?

I poked my head outside the door and spotted it on its end on the far side of the garden - a distance of a least 30 feet. The heavy trampoline had come to rest on a window frame, missing the glass by millimetres. It seemed that the weather had been worse than we thought.

To make matters even worse, our little country cottage had been almost completely destroyed.

George Mahood
@georgemahood

Devastated that our little country cottage has been almost destroyed by #UKStorm2013 :'(

RETWEETS 228 FAVORITES 138

8:08 AM - 28 Oct 2013

Fish and chips with cheese

October 29th

A couple of weeks previously, Sustrans - the charity to promote sustainable transport - opened the first signposted route around the perimeter of Dartmoor National Park. There had been routes around various sections of it before, but until recently, not a complete circuit.

Considering I had holidayed in Devon from a very early age, I knew very little about Dartmoor. We rarely strayed much further than the beach, and Dartmoor National Park was a relative unknown to me. The beach is less of a draw during the colder months, and the possibilities that Dartmoor offers are far more appealing.

The Dartmoor Way, as it has been named, is 95 miles of narrow, hilly back roads, linking the towns of Ivybridge, Bovey Tracey, Okehampton and Tavistock. The idea excited me and I loved the sound of completing it. 95 miles was potentially doable in a single day, but due to the terrain, and the fading light, two days seemed like a more realistic prospect.

My mum and dad are very keen cyclists. They are both retired and go on several cycling holidays a year. Adventures are undoubtedly more fun when shared, and although I see a lot of my parents, it's quite rare that we do anything together, just the three of us.

They were coming down to Devon for the week, so I suggested that we cycle the Dartmoor Way over two days. They liked the sound of the idea, although mum had a few worries, as always, but I told her it would be a doddle, and with a bit of persuasion she agreed to give it a try.

I am not going to claim that it was *Go For a Bike Ride With Your Parents Day*, or *Dartmoor Appreciation Week*. The Dartmoor Way was just too good a resource not to try, and a couple of days with my parents promised to be a lot more fun than celebrating today's holidays: *World Psoriasis Day, National Cat Day* and *Internet Day.*

After a quick smoked salmon and cream cheese bagel for breakfast, we parked the car in Ivybridge, which is a town on the southern tip of Dartmoor. As Dad was topping up the air on his and Mum's bikes he noticed a small bulge in Mum's tyre.

'Do you think it will be a problem?' asked Mum.

'Well it is a little worrying. It could potentially explode at any moment,' he said.

'Oh great, that's just what I want to hear before setting off on a 95 mile bike ride.'

'I'm sure it will be fine. Hopefully it won't explode,' he said reassuringly.

I was riding an old hybrid bike that I was given second hand ten years ago. It was at least ten years old when I got it, so had certainly seen better days; but it had served me well. I wanted to use The Falcon, but it was not the most reliable of bikes, and I decided it would be unfair on my parents to ride such a piece of junk when it could potentially scupper the trip.

After listening to Dad's verdict on Mum's tyre, I took a closer look at my own tyres. I know very little about bikes, but

I was shocked to see that both tyres were in a dreadful state. The front one had a couple of deep splits that ran the entire circumference of the tyre. The cracks almost went through to the inner tube, and it did explain why I had had so many flat tyres recently. The rear tyre wasn't much better. It had hundreds of smaller cracks all around the tyre wall. Even to my untrained eyes, both tyres were perished and certainly unsuitable for cycling any distance, let alone a 95 mile trip into the wilds of Dartmoor.

I gulped but resolutely didn't say anything. It was a bit late to point out that my bike was completely inadequate, so I thought I would take a chance that it would see me through the next two days.

'Everything OK?' asked Dad.

'Yes, absolutely fine. Perfect. Thanks. Let's get going,' I said.

Shortly after 9am we left the car park and soon picked up the first of the Dartmoor Way signs. 50 miles lay between us and Okehampton - our destination for the night - on the northern edge of Dartmoor.

I would like to claim that it was a beautiful, sunny day, but that would be a massive lie. Britain was still experiencing one of the worst storms of the year. Wind and rain had caused huge amounts of damage and disruption the previous day, and the wind was still noticeably strong. We considered cancelling the trip, but knew it was unlikely we would get another chance to do it together this year, so pressed ahead.

We followed the main road east of Ivybridge. At Bittaford, the road climbed steeply up onto the moor. The high hedges on either side of the narrow lanes provided welcome protection from the vicious wind, but it was extremely tough going. We reached the top of the first hill and stopped for the first of many breaks.

After about five miles we reached a section where the entire road was covered in hedge cuttings. There was no avoiding them and I did not hold out much hope of my bike getting through unscathed. As I reached the bottom of a hill, I felt the familiar wobble of the front wheel, and looked down to see the tyre was completely flat.

'Oh, fucking bollocks,' I said to myself as I waited for Mum and Dad to catch up.

'You ok?' asked Mum.

'I thought it would be a miracle if we got through that section without a flat,' I said as they pulled up alongside.

'Oh dear. Have you got a puncture?'

'Yes, but I've got a spare tube so it won't take long,' I said, as I flipped the bike upside down and made a start removing the front wheel. I was feeling smug that I had brought a spare inner tube in case of this eventuality.

I moved the tyre through my fingers, checking for any obvious sign of the cause of the puncture, expecting to find a thorn. I was shocked to see a blunt stick - thicker than a pencil - protruding through one of the many cracks in my perished tyre. I quickly discarded it and tried not to draw further attention to the poor state of my bike.

Putting the new inner tube into place, I then started to inflate it. I had only been going a few seconds when there was an almighty cracking sound and I looked down to see the valve snapped completely in two. We were in the middle of nowhere and I had just snapped the valve off my only spare inner tube.

'What the hell?' I said. 'I only bought that a couple of days ago.'

'Where did you buy it from?' asked Dad.

'EBay,' I sighed. 'I've got a puncture repair kit so I'll just stick a patch on the one with the hole in it.'

'I've got a spare tube,' said Dad. 'I think it should fit your bike, too.'

Whilst I repaired the puncture, Dad put his spare tube in my tyre and inflated it. Less than 20 minutes after the puncture, we were back on the road again and I was relieved not to have held us back too much.

As we reached Buckfastleigh, only a few miles later, I noticed that my rear tyre had started to deflate too. I confessed to my parents about the state of my bike, and that I was in need of a couple of new tyres, otherwise this was going to become an extremely frequent occurrence. Mum knew of a cycle shop in Ashburton, which was about three miles further along the route.

There is an additional section of the Dartmoor Way that crosses the middle of the moor, and we accidentally took this but I thankfully realised our error before we ended up even further from help.

It had taken far longer to get to Buckfastleigh than we had planned, and I didn't want to waste precious time replacing my inner tube, so I cycled all the way to the *Big Peaks* cycle store in Ashburton with a completely flat back tyre. It was totally exhausting, but I just about managed to keep up the pace, knowing that it wasn't doing any good to either my bike or my body.

We pulled up outside the bike shop at 1pm, having covered less than 20 miles in four hours. Thankfully the shop was open and the staff were extremely helpful. I bought two new tyres, plus three new inner tubes (just in case), and my mum bought a new rear tyre to ease her worries.

Our expensive pit-stop coincided with the worst of the weather, as the rain pounded the car park whilst we enjoyed a nice coffee and waited for the repairs to be completed. The staff assured us we would make it to Okehampton in plenty of time, despite only having about four hours of daylight remaining.

The route in the afternoon passed through many idyllic rural villages (I don't think you can get urban villages, can you? Greenwich Village maybe?) But apart from a lovely stretch along a disused railway after Bovey Tracey, the road was either uphill or downhill, and incredibly tough going.

I was impressed with my mum and dad's tenacity on the hills and being 30 years younger than them did not seem to give me any advantage.

On the final stretch into Okehampton, as the sun began to set, the rain pelted our faces making it painful to look anywhere other than directly down towards the front wheel. We pulled into Okehampton wet, tired, wobbly and very much looking forward to a well-deserved beer and some dinner.

We were staying at the White Hart Hotel; a hotel that Ben and I had washed in exchange for dinner, bed and breakfast on the fourth night of our Land's End to John O'Groats trip. On our previous visit, we arrived at the hotel and asked if there was any work that we could do in exchange for somewhere to stay, and the manager wrote us a list, which included washing the outside of the hotel - a job which took us late into the night. We then drank beer until 3am with a Polish pizza chef named Arek in his flat at the top of the hotel.

It was a relief to know that we didn't have to do any cleaning tonight, and that we could eat or drink whatever we liked (providing we paid for it, of course).

I instantly recognised the man who showed us where to lock our bikes. He had been the young deputy-manager when Ben and I had visited, and had been blindfolded by the crazy knife-wielding pizza chef Arek on our previous visit.

'Aren't you going to say anything?' whispered Mum.

'No. He won't remember me. And if he has read my book I doubt he will want to speak to me. I probably didn't paint the White Hart in the best light.'

'Fair enough.'

The pizza restaurant attached to the back of the pub where Arek had worked was still going. It seems that pizza has finally caught on in Okehampton, but unfortunately it was closed on Tuesdays. Arek had not responded to an email that I sent him, so I think he had moved on to pastures new, or perhaps gone into hiding.

After a game of cards, five pints and burger and chips, we all went off to bed.

Before falling asleep, I did manage to quickly celebrate all three of today's holidays (*World Psoriasis Day, National Cat Day* and *Internet Day*) by looking up pictures of cats with psoriasis on the internet. It's not something I would recommend.

October 30th

I woke to my phone's alarm at 7am, feeling rough and regretting that fifth pint. I avoided the ketchup during breakfast after it had exploded over me during our previous visit, and then we climbed onto our bikes to cycle down the western edge of Dartmoor back to Ivybridge.

The cycling was immensely more enjoyable than the previous day; the storm had passed and the sun even made an appearance on a couple of occasions. It was one of the nicest day's cycling I have ever had.

The road climbed steeply up to the old Okehampton train station, where we met the Granite Way. The Granite Way is a cycle trail that follows the old railway line between Okehampton and Lydford. It is a beautiful, flat, traffic-free route that is a cyclist's paradise. On a Wednesday morning at the end of October, we had the entire route to ourselves.

After Lydford, the road skirted around the spectacular church of St. Michael de Rupe in Brentor, perched high on a hill, and then met the Drake's Trail - another beautiful section of disused railway. We must have crossed at least five magnificent viaducts during the day. These extraordinary feats of engineering, built at a time when the machinery was very basic, are now for the sole use of walkers and cyclists.

On one hand, it seemed such a waste of the immense amount of time, money and effort that went into building these railways. On the other, it was fantastic that these former rail routes through rural Britain can now be used for a different means. Sections of railways are being reopened all of the time, as Britain's cycling network continues to expand.

It had been *National Take Your Parents to Lunch Day* a couple of weeks previously, but they were back in Northampton at the time, so I offered to treat them both to a pub lunch today instead. Because we had a time constraint of getting to Ivybridge before dark, they opted for lunch at a bakery in Tavistock instead. After a quick steak pasty and a bag of Haribo, we left the Drake's Trail and the road undulated again up and over the fringe of Dartmoor. Compared to the luxury of the old railway lines, it was exceptionally hard work, but we reached the car park in Ivybridge at about 4pm at the end of two unforgettable day's cycling.

Cycling The Dartmoor Way is a truly memorable experience, and one that I will certainly tackle again.

Create a Great Funeral Day encourages people to take the stress out of organising a funeral by sitting down with loved ones to discuss what sort of a send off we would like. It sounds morbid, but it is actually a very sensible idea.

Rachel and I have very different ideas. I want to be cremated because I'm slightly claustrophobic and don't like the idea of being trapped in a box for eternity. Rachel is not a big fan of burning, and understandably doesn't like the idea of spending eternity as a pile of ash.

For my funeral, I would like my ashes to be put into a firework and set off on a beach, followed by a communal sea swim, whatever the weather, and then a barbecue and beers. If my funeral is in the winter, or on a particularly cold and miserable day, then a sea swim, followed by a few pints and fish and chips at the local pub will suffice. It sounds like a great day. I only wish I could take part.

A few years ago I thought I had invented the greatest idea ever - a company that made fireworks containing cremation ashes. The company was going to be called *Heavens Above* and it was going to make me rich. I then discovered that not only

195

were there companies that already did this, but that one of them was called *Heavens Above*.

Cheese quesadilla with sweet chilli sauce

It was time for me to admit defeat in the battle of *Man vs. Edam*. It didn't matter how much cheese I ate, it kept appearing in larger quantities than before. It was a fight I could never win.

In the battle of Man vs. Edam... Edam won!

October 31st

It was school half term and Rachel's sister and family had come to stay with us for a few days. No school holiday would be complete without a trip to Woodlands.

Woodlands had decked their theme park out for Halloween and rebranded it as a Family Scream Park. With six children aged six and under in tow we set off for a day of fun.

As part of the day, the children all got to carve a pumpkin, and it seemed a little impractical to transport six pumpkins around with us, so I offered to take them back to the car in Kitty's buggy. I piled all six pumpkins into the buggy, and strolled casually back towards the car park. Every child and adult that I passed stared at me in horror as I passed. What was all the fuss about? Had they not seen someone transporting pumpkins in a pushchair before? I then took a look and realised that because of the way I had positioned them, it did look as though I was taking a demonic orange baby for walk.

'She's just feeling a little under the weather,' I said jokingly.

'Ha ha,' laughed one lady, nervously. 'Come along, children. This way.'

I opted to take a shortcut across the grass picnic area between the entrance and the car park, but the grass was a little soggy underfoot so proved hard going with the buggy. The front wheel sank into a particularly soft bit of mud and my momentum caused the pushchair to somersault forwards spilling the six pumpkins across the grass.

'OH MY GOD!' shrieked a lady picnicking nearby with her family.

'Arghhhh,' screamed another, rushing to my aid.

'It's ok, it's ok, they are just pumpkins.'

'Pumpkins?' said the lady. 'Oh thank the lord for that. I thought something terrible had happened to your child.'

'I'm sorry. I was just using the pushchair to get them to the car. No children were harmed.'

'What was that man doing?' asked one of the lady's children, back at her picnic bench.

'I've no idea,' she said. 'Strange man.'

There is mirror maze at Woodlands. It's a maze, made of mirrors, as the name implies, and it features various displays of skeletons, sharks, shipwrecks set amongst lots of mirrors. Outside of the entrance there is a big sign saying 'Mirror Maze', as you would expect it should, and underneath, in smaller writing, it says: *find the lever to unlock the secret of the mirror maze.*

I hadn't noticed the sign before but today Layla did.

'What does that mean, Daddy?' she asked.

'I don't know. It must mean there is a lever in there somewhere that you can pull and then something happens.'

'Come on, let's find it.'

We walked through the maze and there was no sign of it. So we went through again, this time scouring every inch of it for a lever or button that would unlock whatever secret the maze was hiding. Again, we found nothing. It was quite dark in there, so we went through for a third time, using our hands to touch every hidden nook and cranny that even the cleaners never visited.

Nothing.

It was really starting to piss me off. Where was the fucking lever? I was not going to be defeated by a kid's theme park exhibit. We tried one last time but it was fruitless.

'Oh well, maybe we'll find it next time,' said Layla.

'It's so annoying,' I said. 'I really want to find that lever and find out what the secret of the mirror maze is.'

'So do I, but we've looked everywhere. Why don't we ask one of the people who work here?'

'Because that would be cheating! We will find it next time we come.'

'Can we bring torches next time to help us look?'

'Err... yeah... I guess.'

'Ok. Don't forget.'

We didn't get many trick-or-treaters when we lived in Northampton. The first few years after we moved in we had a steady stream, but in recent years the numbers had dwindled. It might be that there weren't as many families living in the area as there once were, or perhaps it was the increased fear and protectiveness of parents.

Rachel answered the door to a group of teenagers on Halloween a few years ago. Layla was too young to go trick-or-treating at the time, but was excited about giving sweets to others, so stood at the door holding a large bowl that we had prepared. The teenagers had made no effort to dress up whatsoever, other than pulling the cords of their hoodies tight. They did look pretty scary to be fair. After shouting 'trick or treat', a mass of hands all dived into the bowl simultaneously, almost emptying the contents in one go. The group then all ran off laughing, whilst Layla stood there looking slightly traumatised.

If it had been me, I would have muttered something to myself about the *'youth of today'* and then quickly closed the door. Not Rachel, she marched into the street and gave chase. She then launched a tirade of abuse to them down the street about how rude and disrespectful they were, as the hooded youths hid behind a van.

Actually, now I think about it, I have just realised why we didn't get many trick-or-treaters in the years after that.

Despite living in the middle of nowhere in Devon this year, we dressed all six cousins up in full fancy dress, and knocked on the door of our landlord's farmhouse across the yard.

They opened the door and were surprised to see them all standing there. Bill has lived in the house all of his life, and these were the first trick-or-treaters that had ever visited. I think that this was something to be proud of.

NOVEMBER

November 1st

My first proper paid experience as a writer came when I worked for a company called *63336 - Any Question Answered*.

I was sitting in a pub with Ben and he told me about a new text service where you could text any question to 63336, and get an answer - all for the cost of £1 (please check their website for current charges before texting. Your house is at risk if you do not keep up repayments. Terms and conditions apply).

'What do you mean '*any question?*' I said.

'ANY question at all. Absolutely anything. Give it a go.'

'Like what sort of thing?'

'Whatever you want. General knowledge. Advice. ANYTHING.'

He pulled out his phone and opened up a new text message. This was in 2005, pre-smartphone, otherwise we could have found the answer to most questions ourselves.

'Err... I don't know...' I said, looking around the bar. 'How about... How much does a pint of Guinness cost at The Picturedrome in Northampton?'

'Ok, well I'm not sure that's the kind of thing they would answer.'

'You said ANY question,' I said. 'The company is called *Any Questions Answered* after all.'

'Fair enough. Let's give it a try,' he said, tapping away at his phone with bleepy buttons.

'How long does it take?' I asked.

'We should get a response soon. I don't think you get charged if they can't answer it.'

A few seconds later the phone rang behind the bar and the barman walked over to answer it. We couldn't hear him over the music and conversation in the pub, but he had a short conversation, hung up the receiver, and carried on drying glasses.

Ben then received a text message a minute later.

'A pint of Guinness in The Picturedrome, Northampton costs £2.80. AQA would like a pint too if you're buying.'

'What the fuck!' I said. 'How did that just happen?'

'See. I told you it was good.'

'Do you think someone phoned the pub?'

'Maybe. It was a bit of a coincidence if not. Excuse me,' Ben called to the barman.

'Yes, buddy. How can I help you?'

'Bit of a random question. When you just spoke to someone on the phone, were they asking about beer prices?'

'Yes. How did you know? They asked how much a pint of Guinness was.'

'Was it a real person? I mean, as opposed to a computer voice?'

'Yes. It was definitely a real voice. She sounded quite fit actually. What was it all about?'

We explained the concept to the barman, who seemed equally impressed as we both were.

'I wonder who these people are,' I said. 'That must be their jobs. To just sit and answer questions all day. Do you think they all work in a sort of call centre, or can you just sit at home in your pants?'

'I don't know. It does sound fun, though.'

'It sounds like my ideal job,' I said. 'As soon as I get home, I'm going to find out more about them and see if I can get a job working for them.'

So that is exactly what I did. I went home, found their website, and found a link to apply to become a 'researcher' and filled in the online form. The following day I received all sorts of forms to fill in, plus a spelling and punctuation test, in which I had to proofread a document (I know what you're thinking. How the hell did I pass that?) I also had to research and provide answers to a set of sample questions, which I was assessed on.

This was in the months after I had quit my job in charity fundraising, and was trying to build a career as a photographer. Needless to say, I had a lot of spare time on my hands. I thought Rachel would be impressed by my ingenuity at applying for such an adaptable job.

'So how much does this job pay?' she asked.

'It's 30p per answer.'

'30p! And how long does a question take to answer?'

'It depends. Some of them are easy and you can select an answer that's already in the database. Others take quite a lot longer to research.'

'How much longer?'

'I don't know. Maybe 15 minutes?'

'FIFTEEN MINUTES? So that's potentially four questions per hour. That's £1.20/hour. It's not the most lucrative of careers is it?'

'No, it's not a career. It's just an opportunity to earn a bit of extra money when I have spare time.'

'You have quite a lot of spare time.'

'Well, it's not going to stop me trying to be a photographer. I can just do this in the evenings. It will be fun.'

I got the job as an Any Question Answered Researcher.

I spent almost a year working for AQA. There weren't many questions sent during the day, so I used to sit on the sofa in the evenings in my pants with my laptop, just as I had always dreamed, answering people's questions.

The questions covered all sorts of areas; often trivia, when a simple Google search would find the answer; sometimes relationship advice when, as a researcher, it was our duty to provide the best possible agony-aunt response in 153 characters. Any question that contained reference to anything illegal, or prohibited, was sent a standard response that stated it was *'not our policy to answer questions of that nature'*, and any excessive questioning by the same number was sent a text reminding them of the charges involved.

I got pretty good at it, and we had regular assessments which I tended to score quite highly on. The better I got, the quicker I became, and the more questions per hour I could answer. Despite this, I was still earning far less than the minimum wage, but it was an experience I enjoyed immensely.

I didn't realise it at the time, but, looking back I think that it was one of the most influential factors in fuelling my desire to write books. I enjoyed the challenge of arranging words into an appealing order. I enjoyed the buzz and excitement at the thought of the reader at the other end smiling, or maybe even laughing, at what I had written. I enjoyed being paid to research things on the internet. But most importantly, I enjoyed sitting in my pants on the sofa and being able to call it work.

Today was *Authors' Day*. A day I should be embracing as technically I am an author. Yet I still don't feel like I belong. I have only published one book. Yes, I am about to publish a second, and am writing my third, but until then I don't see myself as an author. I'm just a bloke who happened to write a book.

I decided to celebrate by sitting around the house in my pants anyway. Perhaps by the time you read this - my third book - I will feel able to call myself an author.

November 2nd

NaNoWriMo has become increasingly popular in recent times. For the last few years I kept seeing the word appear on my Twitter and Facebook timelines, but I didn't have any idea what it was about. It seemed to have some connection to writers, and people writing lots over a certain amount of time, as mentions were often accompanied by a word count or target. I felt like I should know what it was, but the meaning had somehow passed me by, and I was too embarrassed to ask, and too lazy to research it.

Now, as I celebrate these holidays, it is very obvious. *NaNoWriMo* stands for *National Novel Writing Month*.

NaNoWriMo was founded in 1999 by Chris Baty in San Francisco. The idea is participants write an entire 50,000 word novel during the month of November. That's 1667 words per day for the entire month. They don't have to necessarily be good words, and the book doesn't have to be ready for print by December 1st, but the idea is there to encourage writers, or aspiring writers, to sit down and get some words on the page. 21 people took part in the year that it was conceived. This year, it is estimated that 500,000 people will take part.

NaNoWriMo is a brilliant concept, but it has come into a fair bit of criticism over the years. People have suggested that it encourages dross and results in poorly written and badly structured prose. These critics are missing the point. Just because a book is written, doesn't mean that it will start taking up space in a bookshop, or in an Amazon bestseller list. It's more of a personal challenge to allow those that have always wanted to write a novel to feel disciplined enough to actually write it, rather than constantly saying *'I'd love to write a book ONE day'*.

Writing is a discipline, and writing every day might produce a lot of shit (this book is testament to that) but, although it sounds obvious, unless you sit down and actually write, then a book won't ever get written.

In a sense, I have been celebrating *NaNoWriYe* which is *National Novel Writing Year*. The nature of my holiday project is that I have to write something pretty much every day. It has made me far more disciplined, and even when this year is over, I still hope to stick to the habit of writing something each day.

As for celebrating *NaNoWriMo* this year, I decided to celebrate it as best I could, but with a slightly different interpretation of the rules. You are supposed to write a NEW novel from start to finish in the month of November. I was already writing a daily diary of my holiday celebrations, and I confess that I have still not finished writing up Part 1 of this book, which documents the first half of the year. To then add a third novel on top of these would be almost impossible.

So I planned to still write 50,000 words during the month of November, but they wouldn't be for a new book; they would be spread across this book and the unfinished *Every Day Is a Holiday*. The other aim that I set myself was to have Part 1 finished by the end of the month, with the intention of publishing it before Christmas. So, enough waffling, I'd better get writing. Actually, I have written 610 words on how I am going to celebrate *NaNoWriMo*. I'm on a roll. This *NaNoWriMo* is a piece of piss. That's another eleven words there. And another five there.

National Give Up Your Shoulds Day confused me a lot more than it should have. I could not for the life of me work out what 'shoulds' were. I kept reading it as 'showld', and assumed that it must be some sort of shawl or shroud, or perhaps a cross between the two. It would be no problem for me to give them up, as I have never had use for a shawl or shroud anyway. I read descriptions of the day on the internet, and it described getting rid of stress and of being held back and hindered by 'shoulds'. What the hell were these things and how could a scarf cause so many problems? And then I realised how stupid I had been. The word is should. As in should. It rhymes with wood. I had just never seen it written as a plural before, and it completely flummoxed me. I sensibly decided not to mention this stupid error to Rachel and hopefully nobody will ever know. Oh, wait...

The idea of *National Give Up Your Shoulds Day* it to rid yourself of any potential regrets you might have, by thinking of all the things in your life that you 'should' have done and actually doing them. One of the things I will take away from this holiday challenge is the way in which I have had to seize different opportunities. I haven't had nearly as many shoulds as I normally would, because I am doing far more than usual. I am certainly going to give up my shawl and shrouds though.

November 3rd

Less than two months ago Rachel took up running and today she took part in her first ever running event - the Plymouth 10k.

The race started at an unreasonable 8:30am, so we had to wake the children, and put them in the car for 6:30am with a bowl of dry cereal each.

'Why are we having breakfast in the car?' asked Leo.

'Because we are going to watch Mummy in a race, remember?'

'I hope Mummy wins the race,' said Layla.

'I won't win,' said Rachel. 'I just want to finish it. I will be near the end because most people will be much faster than me.'

'Mummy will still get a medal, though,' I added.

'Even if she loses?'

'She won't come last. But even the person that does come last will get a medal.'

'That sounds like a bit of a silly race. What's the point in it being a race if you get a medal for losing?' said Layla.

'Some people will try to win it, but most people will just be running to try and do it the best they can,' I said.

Layla chuffed.

Because of the road closures, we drove around Plymouth for almost an hour trying to get our bearings and find a parking space. In the frantic rush to get all of the children kitted out, I managed to lose Rachel's stopwatch somewhere between the car and the start line. I sprinted half a mile across the city back to the car to try and locate it but was unsuccessful.

'I'm so sorry,' I grovelled to Rachel, back near the start line.

'I was relying on that stopwatch. That was all I had to be able to know how well I am doing,'

'I'm sorry. I don't know where it went. I searched everywhere. Are you sure I didn't give it to you?'

'Yes, I'm sure. You definitely had it. Don't worry about it. It's fine.'

'Oh dear. Well, you did say that you could only run at one speed. So a stopwatch wouldn't really make much difference.'

'That's not the point. It would still be nice to know how I'm doing. I'm just a bit nervous about the whole thing.'

'I know you are, but you'll do brilliantly, I promise,' I said, giving her a big kiss.

Rachel handed me her jumper and hurried off to the start line. The children and I found a spot by the side of the road close to the first kilometre mark. Layla and I had made some banners whilst Rachel was out, and hidden them in the rucksack. I unrolled them and handed one each to the children, and we held them up just as Rachel disappeared past us in a mass of bodies.

'She didn't even see us,' shouted Layla.

'I think she did. Don't worry, we'll make sure she sees us when she comes past again.'

The 10K was an out and back course, meaning that they ran for 5K in one direction, and then turned around and came back along the same route. It was cold and wet so we took shelter in a bus stop and awaited her return. Amusing three young children at the side of the road for an hour was not an easy task. They were all extremely excited about their banners, and stood at the side of the road shouting and waving. To nobody. When the elite runners eventually came into sight after 30 minutes the hysteria increased.

'There's one,' shouted Kitty, when she saw the first runner.

'Oh yes, well spotted,' I said.

'There's two ones,' she said when she saw the second.

We clapped and cheered, and each time I stopped clapping, Kitty and Leo asked me why I had stopped and made me continue. I kept warning them that mummy might not be running past for a little while, but it didn't dampen their enthusiasm.

Leo soon tired of this, however, and then sat on the seat in the bus stop moaning about wanting to go home. Kitty then kept trying to jump off the kerb under the feet of the passing runners. Then, despite my warning about how she would get dizzy, she span around a lamppost continuously until she fell over and hit her head on the seat of the bus stop and screamed. Leo continued to moan, and Layla kept telling me how bored she was.

At last I spotted Rachel coming down the road. She had got to us much quicker than I had anticipated. I shoved a biscuit in Kitty's mouth to stop her crying, put the banner in her hand, encouraged Leo and Layla to the roadside, and we all stood there with our banners as Rachel/Mummy ran past.

I was so proud of her. A few months previously she couldn't even run a few hundred metres without stopping for breath, and now she was on the final half kilometre of ten, in a very, very quick time. And more importantly, she looked like she was enjoying it.

We hurried across to meet her outside the finishers' enclosure where she proudly showed us her medal, even though Layla thought she didn't deserve it having not won the race. I had never seen Rachel so excited, and I felt far more emotional than I did after finishing any of my own runs.

'I loved it,' she said. 'I really loved it. It was so lovely to see you all at the end there with your banners. What a nice surprise!'

A few minutes later she received a text with her finishing time. She was hoping to complete it in under 1 hour 15 minutes.

'54 minutes!' I said, 'That's incredible. Well done you. See, you were better off without a stopwatch after all.'

'I'm proud as punch for you,' I said in the car on the way home.

'Aww, thanks.'

'You did so well. You must be as fit as a fiddle. I think you gave it 110%. What is your medal made of?'

'I don't know.'

'Because all that glitters is not gold.'

'Right...'

'You're the apple of my eye. The light of my life.'

'Why are you talking like that?'

'It's *Cliche Day*.'

'Oh goody.'

'Want any more? Because I've got more than you can shake a stick at.'

November 4th

Chicken Lady Day is said to have been created in 2001 by President Bush to honour the work of Dr. Marthenia 'Tina' Dupree. Dupree worked for a chicken restaurant (hence the nickname *'The Chicken Lady'*) as Director of Community Relations and Training, and through her work with the community, she helped and inspired thousands of people to improve their lives and to live their dreams.

Strangely, the notion of a Chicken Lady immediately made me think of a Northampton news story that I read just a few days ago. The news story in question was very unfortunate for the lady involved, but there was something about the headline that seemed to capture the entire essence of Northampton in one short sentence.

Girl Dressed as a Chicken Punched in the Face by Boy Outside Northampton Discount Store.

It is surely one of the greatest headlines ever written. It was completely irrelevant that she was standing outside a discount store when she was punched, but it somehow added to the story, and it weirdly made me feel slightly nostalgic again about the mean streets of Northampton. I dedicated this year's *National Chicken Lady Day*, not just to Dr. Dupree, but to the Chicken Girl who was punched in the face by a boy outside a Northampton discount store.

November 5th

'Remember, remember the 5th of November' is such a rubbish mnemonic. The word FIFTH is the important part of the rhyme, as this is the date that you are being asked to remember, twice. But this part of the sentence can be replaced by any other date and it still makes perfect sense. *'Remember, remember the 9th of November'*. It's useless. They should invent a rhyme where 5th is the rhyming word so that it cannot be forgotten.

There are plenty of words that rhyme with fifth: pith, Smith, Penrith... err... Sith? Actually, that's all I can think of.

Remember, remember November the fifth,
Oranges are delicious, except for the pith.

Maybe we should stick with the original rhyme.

Bonfire Night, or *Guy Fawkes Night*, is such a well recognised event on the calendar in the UK, that people never forget it anyway. It wasn't until this holiday project that it dawned on me that *Bonfire Night* is not really celebrated elsewhere in the world. Some countries do, but it is predominantly a British thing. It does, after all, commemorate the date on which Guy Fawkes was caught guarding explosives beneath the House of Lords, in an attempt to destroy parliament and King James I.

Bonfire Night was always one of the highlights of the year when I was a child. My mum and dad were part of the committee that organised our local one, so I was always involved with helping to build the bonfire, which usually involved being towed around a muddy field on a trailer behind a tractor. Also, my dad was usually one of the select few to be responsible for lighting the fireworks.

'You see that man in the hi-vis jacket and the torch over on the ridge?' I would say to my friends.

'Yeah.'

'That's my dad,' I said, proudly.

'Woah. He's so coooool.'

'I know.'

The post-Bonfire Night clear up the following morning was even better. We would try to bring the still smouldering embers of the bonfire back to life, and burn all of the paper cups littering the ground. We then got to scour the field to find as many of the firework shells as we could. Ah, those were the days; building bonfires, playing with fireworks. What a childhood.

As for actual firework displays, I'm a big believer in short, sharp displays; lots of fireworks, lots of impact, and then all over. In recent years, due to advances in electronic ignition systems, there have been a few firework displays that have hit the headlines because of malfunctions. San Diego had a spectacular failure in 2012, but my favourite was the one in

Oban, Scotland, in 2011. Due to a mistake, 6000 fireworks - that's about 30 minutes worth - all detonated in less than a minute. I wasn't there, but I've watched the video on YouTube several times, and it is by far the best firework display I have ever seen. I wish all displays were like that.

This year we celebrated Bonfire Night at a firework display in a nearby village. Unfortunately, the fireworks were not electrically controlled, so they all went off at nice regular intervals, but it was fairly short and sweet. I still did look over at the man lighting the fireworks with the hi-vis jacket and the torch, and think *'Woah, he's so coooool.'*

Maybe one day I'll be able to light fireworks, when I grow up.

November 6th

All of the changes from the past few months seemed to have affected Leo's behaviour. Moving house and starting pre-school had contributed to him being particularly stroppy and irritable. He was often prone to outbursts and tantrums, but today's one was especially bad and defied any form of reasoning. It involved a huge amount of tears, screaming, kicking walls, slamming doors and lying on the carpet banging fists. And that was just Rachel. By the time the children were in bed, we had almost reached breaking point.

Thankfully the holidays came to the rescue yet again. It was *Nachos Day*. Nachos are Rachel's favourite food in the whole world.

Nachos originated in Mexico in the city of Piedras Negras, on a stormy night in 1943. I don't know that it was a stormy night, but it makes the story more exciting, so I'm going to go with it. On this incredibly stormy night, with hurricane strength winds, and fork lighting striking the ground all around them, the wives of some U.S. soldiers stationed at nearby Fort Duncan, arrived at the Victory Club restaurant after the kitchen had already closed for the evening. Employee Ignacio 'Nacho' Anaya agreed to provide them with some food, based on what food he had left in the kitchen. He cut some tortillas into triangles, added some cheese, heated it up, and added sliced jalapeños. He called the dish '*Nachos Especiales*'. The popularity of his dish quickly spread throughout Mexico and Texas, and Ignacio Anaya went on to open his own nacho restaurant, and a bronze plaque commemorates his achievement in the city of Piedras Negras. Over the years, various other toppings have been added, including salsa, refried beans, guacamole and soured cream.

We had a huge plate of nachos for dinner, and thanks to Ignacio Anaya, our evening was saved.

November 7th

Movember has become one of the most widely recognised and observed holidays in the world. The idea was hatched, as all great ideas are, in a pub. A group of friends in Australia decided to grow moustaches for the month of November, to help raise awareness for prostate cancer. The idea quickly spread from Australia to countries throughout the world, thanks in part to social media and celebrity partakers. I had always had a reason or excuse to trim my beard during the month. Not this year. This year I would of course be taking part. My dilemma was that I had a wedding on 9th November, and at my pre-wedding meeting, the bride happened to mention that she had requested to all the male guests that they didn't have a moustache at her wedding. This did seem a little bit bridezilla initially, but I could see her point. In years to come, when people looked through their album, and many of the male guests had wispy moustaches, it might look like she got married on the set of a 1970s German porn film.

I knew that I would not be in the wedding photos, so my moustache should not matter, but I didn't want to draw attention to myself and I'd rather not be the one to disrespect the bride's wishes. As a compromise, I decided not to shave at all until after the wedding on the 9th, and from then on, I would allow my moustache to flourish.

November 9th

Today's date, 9/11/13 is a mathematical phenomenon (perhaps that is over-hyping it somewhat). It was the last time this century that the date will consist of three consecutive odd numbers. It only happens five times each century. The date is celebrated by geeks across the world as *Odd Day*.

Americans write the month first, so the last *Odd Day* of the century in the USA was celebrated on 11th September this year. Ron Gordon, a maths enthusiast from California, gets extremely excited about dates like this. He advises that the best and simplest way to celebrate the day is just to tell people about it, and help spread the word about this quirky phenomenon.

So that's what I'm doing. I am telling you all about it. Unfortunately, by the time you read this, *Odd Day* will be over and the next one won't be until 1st March, 2105, by which time almost all of us will be long dead.

But don't worry, Ron is already preparing celebrations for *Trumpet Day* on 2/2/22, because when spoken aloud it sounds like a trumpet apparently (it really doesn't, Ron). So, put the date in your diary (if you have a weird 9 year diary) and I'll look forward to celebrating *Trumpet Day* with you all then.

November 10th

To give Rachel a bit of peace and quiet, I offered to take the children to Woodlands for the day. Layla thoughtfully reminded me that I had promised to take a torch with us on our next visit.

All of our smaller torches were missing batteries, so I had to take the big torch. It is basically an industrial searchlight. Perhaps a little bit extreme to be taking to a kid's theme park, but it was all I had. We needed to find that fucking lever.

'Right, here we go,' I said to Layla, Leo, and Kitty outside the mirror maze. 'This is it. Let's find that lever once and for all.'

Halfway through the maze, Layla announced she didn't want to be there anymore.

'I want to get out. I'm scared.'

'What do you mean you're scared?'

'I'm scared. I don't like it.'

'I'm scared too,' said Leo, who had been perfectly fine up until that point.

'And me,' said Kitty.

'But you've all been in loads of times,' I said.

'I know. But we don't want to be here today.'

'But I've got this big torch this time. How can you be scared?'

'I don't know but we are. Can we wait at the end while you find the lever?'

'Ok, but don't go any further than the exit door, ok?'

I walked slowly through the maze, on my own, shining the spotlight into every corner of the darkness, pressing and pulling everything that could potentially be a lever.

217

Around one of the corners I bumped into a couple with their young son. They looked at me oddly as I accidentally blinded them with my spotlight. I must have looked a strange sight; a moustached man, alone in a child's maze, with an industrial sized torch, scouring every inch of the wall.

'Sorry,' I said, turning off the torch. 'I'm just trying to find the lever to unlock the secret of the mirror maze. Have you seen it?'

'Nope, sorry,' they said nervously, and kept walking.

After another thorough search, I left through the Exit door dejectedly.

'Did you find it, Daddy? Did you find the lever?'

'No,' I said, gritting my teeth and trying to stay calm.

'Where can it be?' said Layla. 'We will have to ask someone now. We've tried everything.'

'I think maybe we will.'

It pained me to admit defeat, but I felt like I had done everything I possibly could. I could not have searched that damn maze any more thoroughly. If there was a secret lever, then it deserved to be hidden forever. The secret of the mirror maze certainly did not want to reveal itself easily. I decided to swallow my pride and ask a member of staff.

A few minutes later, a ranger was passing on his golf buggy and I flagged him down.

'Excuse me. Could you possibly tell us where the lever is to unlock the secret of the mirror maze? We give up.'

'What lever?' he said blankly.

'There's a bit on the Mirror Maze sign that says *find the lever to unlock the secret of the mirror maze*' or something like that,' I said, trying to disguise the fact that I knew it word for word.

'I've never noticed that before. Sorry. Try one of the older members of staff. I haven't worked here that long.'

During the course of the day, I asked a total of SIX members of staff. Each one told me that they had never heard of it before.

'BUT IT SAYS IT ON THE SIGN!' I said in desperation. 'Surely I can't be the only person to have ever looked for it?'

'I think you are, Sir. Sorry,' said one of them.

Later in the day, I made the mistake of asking one of the men I had already asked earlier in the day.

'I think we had this conversation earlier,' he said. 'I'm sorry, I still don't know where the lever is? Have you asked at reception?'

'Yes! I've asked everywhere. Nobody knows where the DAMN LEVER IS.'

'Come on, Daddy. I think it's time we went home now,' said Layla, taking me by the arm. 'It doesn't matter about the lever. Some mysteries are best left unsolved.'

November 15th

My grandma's fridge was legendary. By legendary, I mean revolting. She used to put any leftovers in the fridge, uncovered, until either they were eaten, or until they had decomposed to nothing. She had a collection of jarred foods that had been there since well before best before dates were even invented.

For some reason, she saw it as my calling to be the one to clean out her fridge and food cupboards when I visited. The problem was that she didn't trust me with the contents of her fridge, and so sat next to me in a supervisory role, telling me, as I tried to dispose of 30 year old jars of piccalilli, that it was perfectly fine and that she had planned to use it that very evening.

I was rarely allowed to throw anything out. Occasionally, for plates of food, or bowls of unidentified matter that had developed their own biodiversity, I had to distract her by pointing to something on the other side of the room, before slipping the offending item into the bin.

The only thing worse than my grandma's fridge, was my grandma's freezer. She had an obscenely large chest freezer. The type usually used to hide dead bodies in horror films. There was no risk of finding a dead body in her freezer, however, as every inch of space was filled. Not all with food, though. Mostly with ice.

The freezer was fairly old, and had clearly not been defrosted since the day it was bought. The ice was so thick around the sides that it almost met in the middle, resulting in a post-box sized gap through which my grandma deposited food. The frost wasn't as bad towards the bottom of the freezer so there was an area where food had accumulated over the years. Once food had been posted through this hole, there was no way of ever getting it back.

My grandma was notorious at making her visitors 'useful' and after a brief hello she would launch in to her pre-rehearsed 'Now, George. I've got this list of jobs for you' at which point she would unfold an A4 sheet of paper, on which she had written on both sides.

I once turned up unannounced for a surprise visit, and rather than being delighted to see me, she was irritated that I had not given her time to plan a list of chores. Her lists were always diverse: rearranging the hundreds of pictures on her walls, cleaning the cages of her guinea fowl, scrubbing the patio of all of their excrement and cleaning her car with the only cleaning implements available - a small toothbrush and a bottle of washing up liquid.

But no job will ever compare to the defrosting of that freezer - a job that was assigned to me on one particular visit. It is a day I will remember for the rest of my life.

I genuinely had to use a hammer and chisel to break through the top crust, and then a shovel to remove the vast quantities of ice inside the freezer. At the very bottom I found all sorts of obscure items; there was a huge number of prawns - loose - just scattered amongst the other items. There were mussels, individual sausages, random lumps of meat, peas. It was like she had tipped in the contents of a giant paella dish. Come to think of it, she probably had. I also found two pigs trotters, just sitting neatly at the bottom next to a bag of chips.

'Oh, good. I'd been wondering where those had got to,' she said when I tried to throw them out.

'Wondering since 1983?' I muttered.

But the random food was not the most extraordinary thing in that freezer. It was the pillars of bowls, and empty ice cream containers, that my grandma had filled with stock, stewed fruit, or sauces and then put directly into the freezer, in the uncovered bowl, directly on top of the previous container that had been placed there. Because of the small gap which they had been passed through, these bowls and containers were not stacked level and the contents of each vessel had spilled out over the sides before it had a chance to freeze properly. It is no exaggeration to say there were at least 30 different containers stacked in several rickety frozen towers. The contents were completely unidentifiable. I'm sure when she placed them in the freezer she assumed she would remember what each was, but the reality was that even if she had been able to retrieve them from the depths, through the tiny post-box sized hole, they all just looked like brown mush once frozen anyway.

'I think we can throw out most of these,' I said. 'You must be running short of bowls and containers with all of these in here.'

'Don't be silly. We can't get rid of those. Those stocks are delicious. If you just stack them as neatly as you can I will use them all.'

'Ok then,' I said, despairingly.

'Keep a couple of them out. I'll use them for dinner tonight.'

'Which ones? They all look the same.'

'It doesn't matter. I'll be able to work out what they are when I have a proper look.'

This was a lie. She cooked a delicious roast chicken with vegetables for dinner, but, what she thought was gravy, turned out to be stewed gooseberries, although it actually worked surprisingly well.

She served ice cream for pudding, but I declined the offer of fish stock as an accompaniment.

Today was *National Clean Out Your Refrigerator Day*. The day was created to encourage people to sort out their fridges; to get back into the depths of their shelves and drawers and see what scary items lurk there. After all of the experiences of my grandma's fridge and freezer, nothing scares me anymore.

I pulled out the drawers of ours and found a few offending items: a cucumber that had turned to water, a bunch of celery that was so wilted that it couldn't stand upright, a yoghurt that had leaked and stuck itself to the back of the fridge like a limpet, and a jar of strawberry jam with a luxurious blanket of furry mould on top. Most of the jars were past their best before date, but they all looked perfectly edible, so I didn't throw too much out.

I then decided to see how bad the freezer was. There were no pigs trotters, but there were plenty of loose items in the bottom of the drawer, and four pots of stock/gravy/stewed fruit were stacked on one of the shelves. I was certain when I put them in there that I would remember what they were, but looking at the containers of brown mush I had absolutely no idea. There was no getting away from it; I was turning into my grandma.

Hidden at the very back of the freezer, sandwiched between a pizza and a packet of fish fingers, I found £50.

November 16th

It was another rainy weekend, so we paid yet another visit to Woodlands. We had already got our money's worth from the annual passes in the first two months, but I still hadn't quite got over the elusive lever in the mirror maze. It was *National Day of Play*, which I took to be a sign that I should have just one last look. It was also *National Button Day*, which is a day dedicated to people who collect buttons (the freaks). However, I chose to interpret this as a day to find the button in the mirror maze. Yes I know it's a lever and not a button, but it's pretty much the same thing and I was so desperate to find that bloody lever, alright? Now leave me alone.

'Do you want to go in the mirror maze?' I asked Layla casually after we had flashed our annual passes at the main entrance.

'Daddy, I think it's time that you forgot about the mirror maze. Just let it go. Please'

'I won't look for the lever. I promise. We'll just walk through it.'

'Of course you will look. I bet that's the only reason that you've brought us to Woodlands today.'

'As if! I honestly won't look. Let's go through it once, ok?'

'Ok, but you'd better not look.'

As we approached the entrance I subtly looked at the sign and noticed instantly that something was different.

The bit about the lever was gone.

It had been covered over with a piece of white plastic. My interrogations had clearly made it up the chain to management, and evasive action had been taken. I didn't know whether to be disappointed or elated. It was a relief that this meant the lever no longer existed, but it was a shame that I would never get a chance to see what secrets the mirror maze offered. I imagined various members of staff reporting back to head office about a crazed visitor obsessing over a lever, and the maintenance crew being dispatched immediately to remove all evidence that it ever even existed. Despite the knowledge that the secret was now gone for good, I felt strangely victorious.

'Good riddance, stupid lever,' I laughed, as I walked through the entrance.

November 17th

It was the day of the Cornish Marathon. I had done a little training but nowhere near as much as I hoped. But it was not about the running. It was all about the hoodie and the pasty.

For each of the marathons I had previously completed, I relied heavily on my stopwatch. I monitored each mile rigorously to make sure I kept to my target. This had proved successful for my first three marathons, but during my fourth - the glamorous location of Milton Keynes - the wheels came off completely. Not literally, that would have been cheating. I realised midway through the race that I hated running and didn't care in the slightest how long it took me. I just wanted the damn thing to be over. I ended up walking a lot of it, but once the burden of my target time had gone, I did feel a huge sense of relief.

For today's Cornish Marathon, I decided to take this even further and deliberately left my stopwatch at home, so that I could just run at the speed I wanted to, rather than be governed by the stopwatch. It had inadvertently worked for Rachel, so I thought I would try it for myself.

Rachel offered to come and cheer me on, but I managed to discourage her. The only thing grimmer than running a marathon would be standing on the side of the road with three young children, for potentially five hours, in the hope that they would see me pass.

The race itself was as tough as expected. The scenery was awe-inspiring, though. The route meandered up and down parts of Bodmin Moor, followed rivers swollen with recent rain, climbed valleys and tiptoed through charming little villages.

I felt surprisingly good for the first 22 miles, considering my lack of training, and how brutal the route was. Nothing could prepare me for the last few miles, though, as the road began to climb, and climb, and climb. It was reassuring to see others walking, so I too decided that this stretch had beaten me.

The last half mile was downhill, but the hills had taken their toll so much on the legs that even this section was difficult. All around me runners were hobbling down the final hill with limbs made from jelly. My legs felt like they belonged to someone else, but I managed to clumsily jog the last few hundred metres and finished in a time of 4h 17m, which was exactly the same time that it took me to run around the relatively flat and trouble-free Milton Keynes. It was infinitely more pleasurable not having a stopwatch, too.

The hoodie was a welcome sight, but I felt so sick after the run, that it was nearly an hour before I managed to take a bite from the pasty, by which point it was stone cold.

While I was getting changed, I got chatting to an elderly man with long grey hair named Danny Kay. He had finished his 499th marathon, and was due to complete his 500th at Pisa the following month on the date of his 72nd birthday.

'500 marathons?' I asked. 'That's insane. You must have been running all of your life?'

'Not at all. I did my first marathon when I was in my 40s. I didn't do too many for the first few years either, but then I got the bug.'

He really was an inspiration. And he beat me by about 10 minutes.

On February 3rd this year I unfriended Ian Stewart on Facebook to celebrate *Dump Your Significant Jerk Day*. This backfired on me when I bumped into him in the park a few months later. We became Facebook friends again that same evening.

Today was *Unfriend Day*. Could I possibly unfriend Ian Stewart again? He was still fairly annoying and I hadn't seen him since that day at the park. I lived 250 miles away from him now so the chances of bumping into him were far slimmer, but it still didn't make it any easier. I started trawling through my friends again to find another candidate, but I just kept returning to Ian. I had to unfriend SOMEONE, and it wasn't fair to remove anyone else. It had to be him. I clicked '*unfriend*' and dumped him from my life again. This time it would be for good.

November 20th

It was *National Book Awareness Week*. Book Awareness? Surely everyone is aware of books. Even those that don't read books, at least know they exist.

How would I celebrate this momentous week-long holiday?

Over the past few weeks I had the self-imposed *NaNoWriMo* deadline looming over me to get *Every Day Is a Holiday* finished by the end of the month. As the 30th slipped ever closer, it was looking more and more unlikely that it would be complete in time.

I celebrated *National Book Awareness Week* by making myself aware that my book would not be out next month. Instead, I would do as much as I could in the next few months and then publish *Every Day Is a Holiday* sometime in the New Year. I felt better already.

November 22nd

Rachel handed her CV to the local primary school during the first week of term. They thanked her, and told her they would keep her details and be in contact if they needed a supply teacher. She had not heard from them. Late last night the head teacher phoned asking if she could cover a class today, and she gladly agreed.

'Are you sure you're happy to do the school-run and have Kitty for the day?' she said.

'Absolutely. We'll be fine.'

'What will you do?'

'We'll think of something.'

Go For a Ride Day is a celebration of the freedom that transportation has provided us. Kitty and I celebrated with a very short bike ride. We didn't plan for it to be so short, but she chose to wait until I had slogged to the top of a nearby hill to complain that she was cold in her bike seat, needed the toilet, and wanted to go home.

Rachel's first day of supply teaching was a huge success and she returned home full of energy and enthusiasm, hoping that she would be asked again soon.

Layla was increasingly desperate for her first tooth to fall out. Today she wrote a letter to the tooth fairy asking for her help.

'I'm not sure the tooth fairy is able to help teeth fall out,' I said.

'Why not? That's her job.'

'I thought it was her job to collect the teeth that have already fallen out?'

'Well surely she should be able to help them fall out, too?'

'Maybe. But how will she see the letter if she doesn't have a tooth to collect from under your pillow?'

'She checks under all pillows every night. Then she just leaves money if there is a tooth. She'll find my letter when she's doing her rounds.'

'I see. And if she does get your letter, how are you imagining that she will help pull your tooth out?'

'I don't know. Get her friends to help her maybe?'

'It's worth a try,' I said.

I didn't know quite how to proceed. If I left the letter where it was then Layla would think that the tooth fairy had not paid a visit. If I took the letter, she would be sad that the tooth fairy had not removed her tooth. I was slightly tempted to sneak into her room in the night, and forcibly remove the tooth as Layla wished, but she was bound to wake up.

Instead, I typed up a quick letter from the tooth fairy on my computer, printed it out, and swapped it with the one under her pillow.

Dear Layla,

Thank you for your lovely letter.
Your tooth will come out in time. There is no need to rush. Please be patient.

Lots of love

The Tooth Fairy

November 23rd

Layla was delighted with her letter and insisted on taking it with her to a friend's birthday party to show everyone. When I picked her up later in the day she had a miserable look on her face.

'What's wrong?' I asked.

'Did Mummy write that letter from the tooth fairy?'

'No. Why?'

'All of my friends said she did. They just laughed at me.'

'How come? Don't they believe in the tooth fairy?'

'Of course they believe in her. They just said that the tooth fairy writes tiny little letters in pen. She doesn't have a computer or a printer.'

'Really?' I said, annoyed with myself for making such a schoolboy error. 'Well maybe it was difficult for her to handwrite so many letters each night. Maybe she decided to get a computer to speed things up a bit?'

'But how could she type all of that on a computer and carry a big piece of paper? She's only tiny. It doesn't make sense.'

'I don't know how she did it. But she did. If she is strong enough to carry a tooth then she can carry a piece of paper.'

'Tell me the truth, Daddy. Did Mummy write it?'

'NO! Mummy did not write the letter,' I said, slightly annoyed that she would only think of it as a job that Mummy could do.

'Humph.'

Thankfully she didn't mention the letter again.

'I bought some cranberries,' I said to Rachel back at the house. 'Would you like one?'

'Thanks,' she said, taking a handful.

'Hey! I asked if you would like one. Put the rest back.'

'Ha ha, funny. Why are you being so tight with the cranberries?'

'Because today is *National Eat A Cranberry Day*. That's A cranberry. Not CRANBERRIES.'

'Oh well. You're the one who is supposed to be celebrating these holidays. I've just made up my own day - *Eat Cranberries By the Handful Day*. Oh look, it's today! That's lucky,' she said, taking another handful.

'You're no fun,' I said, slipping a single cranberry into my mouth.

November 24th

We had lived in Devon for three months and Rachel already has a big network of friends. She would go over to people's houses regularly for 'play dates' (with Kitty, obviously), out for coffee, and to various mums and tots groups.

I was still mateless. I didn't mind, to be honest, and I had not made an effort to make new friends. Men are so much crapper at making friends than women are. Mums in particular seem to be great at chatting to other mums, and then suddenly they've arranged a coffee morning. Dads just stand awkwardly at the school gate trying to avoid eye contact with anyone else, and then glancing at their phones regularly so that they don't look too lonely.

Things changed today. I had been asked if I wanted to play football on Sunday mornings. Did I want to play FOOTBALL? Hell yeah! It had been the longest period I had ever gone without playing weekly football since I was a young child. I missed it more than I thought I would.

I was invited to join a group of guys who played at 9am every Sunday. Back when I used to play Sunday football, a

10:30am kick off seemed ridiculously early. Since having children, 9am is considered quite late in the day.

It was a very informal game, with a group of really nice blokes, all keen to have a kick-about on a Sunday morning. It was like a missing part of me had been found. Playing football definitely helped me feel more like me again. I felt like a man.

It was *Celebrate Your Unique Talent Day*, and I would like to claim that Mahood was ON FIRE at football again, but unfortunately those days were long gone. Mahood was little more than the partially burnt, damp remains of a newspaper.

November 25th

The phone rang during breakfast. It was the local head teacher again, asking Rachel if she could teach today and tomorrow.

'Are you sure you don't mind looking after Kitty for both days?'

'Not at all. We'll have a great time.'

'But haven't you got lots of work to catch up on and writing to do?'

'Nah, it's fine. I'm not too concerned.'

'Thank you. You're being very relaxed about it all.'

'Well, it is *Blasé Day*. They must have been really impressed with you on Friday. That's three school days in a row.'

'They are probably just really desperate.'

'Or maybe they realised what a wonderful teacher you are.'

'Is it *Say Something Nice To Your Wife For A Change Day*, too?'

'Of course not. You ARE a wonderful teacher, a wonderful wife, and a wonderful mother.'

'Are you feeling ok?'

November 28th

Why is it that in the UK we only seem to celebrate harvest festivals in primary schools and churches? And our 'celebration' consists of donating a couple of old tins of baked beans. The Americans have *Thanksgiving*, which is basically just a harvest festival, but WAY better.

We should adopt *Thanksgiving* over here, and turn our miserable pathetic harvest festivals into something worth celebrating.

Thanksgiving also serves as the official start of the 'holiday season'. It seems to be accepted in the US and Canada that *Thanksgiving* marks the start of the festive period that carries on until New Year.

There is no such distinction here in the UK, and people never know when they are allowed to officially start getting excited about Christmas. Most of us fall into one of two basic camps: those who are annoyingly overly-enthusiastic about Christmas (*'only 187 sleeps to go'* - you know who you are!). Then we have people like me, who are notoriously bah-humbug about Christmas. I wouldn't dare get excited about Christmas (at least, not openly) until about December 21st.

If, however, we celebrated *Thanksgiving* at the end of November, I would be very happy to turn Christmas into a month-long festive season. Come on, let's do this! It's time to upgrade our sorry harvest festivals. It's time we too celebrated *Thanksgiving*.

Rachel was very excited about the idea of us celebrating Thanksgiving and so we decided to cook a big 'traditional' family meal with all the trimmings.

I spent *Thanksgiving* in 2000 in the US with a friend. We didn't realise it was *Thanksgiving* until we tried to call at a fast-food restaurant and it was closed. Thankfully, Walmart was open, so we bought a tub of cold fried chicken, which we sat and ate in the car park. Sorry, I mean parking lot.

We then had to contend with all the happy faces of families, as they walked back to their cars, laden with groceries and last minute *Thanksgiving* purchases. They all looked at each other and then to us as if to say: '*look at those poor boys having to spend Thanksgiving in a Walmart parking lot, eating cold fried chicken.*' We too started to feel slightly sorry for ourselves. To us, it was just a normal Thursday in November, but it was also a swift reminder that we were a long way from our home and our families.

I took Kitty to the park for a few hours in the morning, because that is what we traditionally do on *Thanksgiving*. After I had strapped her into her car seat to head home I heard a voice behind me.

'Excuse me. Do you know if the buses to Colsworth are running today?'

I turned around to see an elderly lady standing there. She was immaculately dressed and holding her handbag, but was not wearing a coat, which was slightly surprising considering how cold it was.

'I'm afraid I don't know. Where do they normally go from?'

'They usually leave from the bus stop just over there,' she said, pointing towards the town.

'It's Thursday today. Do you know if they run on Thursday afternoons?'

'I don't, dear. I came to visit my brother in his house just over there, but he's not feeling too well so I have decided to get the bus home.'

'Colsworth did you say?'

'Yes, dear. Do you know it?'

'Yes, I know where it is. It's not too far, is it?'

'No, dear. I'll wander over to see if there are any buses.'

She started to walk off and looked a little unsteady on her feet. The bus stop was about 1/4 of a mile from where we were standing, and I was worried she might get there and find there were no buses.

'Would you like me to give you a lift home?' I asked.

'Really? Would you mind, dear? That would be awfully kind of you.'

'Not at all. That's no problem. It is *Thanksgiving*, after all.'

'It that today?'

'Yes, we can't have you waiting around for the bus on your own at *Thanksgiving*.'

'Well, dear, if you insist. This is awfully kind of you.'

I walked around to the passenger side and opened the door for her. I was just about to help her into the seat when a lady in a nurse's uniform came running around the corner.

'Ethel, there you are!' she said. 'We were worried about you.'

She then turned to look at me. 'And who are you? Where were you planning on taking her?'

'I'm really sorry. I had just offered her a lift home.'

'A lift home? Just like that? She lives in the care home around the corner. She's not supposed to be out by herself.'

'I didn't... I... sorry,' I stuttered.

'You should be ashamed of yourself.'

The nurse just glared at me, took Ethel by the arm and led her briskly away. Well, as briskly as Ethel possibly could, which wasn't particularly briskly.

'Who was that lady?' asked Kitty in the car.

'I thought she was lost. But it turns out her house is just around the corner so that other lady came to look after her. '

I told Rachel the story when I got home, because I felt like I had been very foolish.

'But you were only trying to help,' she said.

'If I had known there was a care home next door then I would obviously have checked there first.'

'It sounds like the nurse was just embarrassed by her mistake and so took it out on you.'

'Yes, maybe.'

'Although, in her defence, you do look quite dodgy with that moustache.'

'Oh shit, I'd forgotten about my moustache. Do you think it would have been different if I'd been clean shaven?'

'Possibly. Although you had Kitty with you. At least she would have given you a bit more credibility.'

'She was in the car. The nurse wouldn't have seen her.'

'Oh, well that changes everything. A strange-looking moustachioed man, hanging around at a children's playground, trying to coax old ladies into his car. I'm surprised she didn't call the police.'

After we had sat down for a thoroughly enjoyable *Thanksgiving* dinner, my little incident at the park was soon forgotten.

DECEMBER

December 1st

Today was all about getting rid of my moustache. It was not something I will be making into a regular feature of my face. It was itchy, annoying, prickly, ginger, and it caused much hilarity from people I met. Rachel didn't look at me for the entire month of November, I was looked at suspiciously when alone in a mirror maze, and I nearly got arrested for abducting an old lady.

Movember has got its priorities all wrong. Forget prostate cancer; it should be raising awareness for all of the brave and courageous men who have a moustache all year round. Those are the real heroes. Stay strong, guys.

December 2nd

The phone rang at 5:00pm. It was Doug.
'He's gone missing again,' he said.

I knew instantly he was talking about Basil.

'Oh no. How long for?'

'He had his breakfast here this morning, George, and I haven't seen him since.'

'I'm sure he's just gone for a wander. I wouldn't worry too much about it. He's been missing less than a day.'

'He's definitely gone, George. I've already phoned Radio Northampton and they are going to do an announcement.'

'Oh, right...' I said, slightly taken aback. It did seem slightly ludicrous that Doug would be worried about Basil after only a few hours, but I knew that he was very tuned in to Basil's daily routine so probably had cause for concern.

'George, would you possibly be able to do me some of those MISSING posters like you did before and send them to me? As you know we don't have a computer and I wouldn't know where to start.'

'Yes, of course. That's no problem. Perhaps it would be best to wait until tomorrow, just in case he comes back during the night.'

'I know he's gone, George.'

'Ok, well we've missed today's post anyway, so if he's still missing tomorrow then I'll send the posters to you first class, so you'll have them the following day. Is that ok?'

'That would be great, thanks.'

'I hope he comes back soon.'

'Me too, kiddo. Me too.'

December 3rd

Having owned our house in Northampton, the intention was always to buy a house down in Devon. After being laughed out of the bank by a mortgage advisor, we realised that renting was

239

our only viable option. We thought this would only be temporary, and would buy our own place soon.

Having lived in our house for a few months, and loved the place and its location, we had got used to the idea of renting, and it is definitely something we could see ourselves doing long-term. Today was *Roof Over Your Head Day*; a day to remind us of how lucky we are to have somewhere to live, when many all over the world are far less fortunate.

Doug phoned at lunchtime to say that Basil was still missing.

'I will print off 100 posters for you and put them in the post today,' I said.

'Thanks George. You're a star.'

'Is it just posters that you need? Do you want me to print any flyers to put through people's doors?'

'No thanks. Just the posters will be fine.'

December 4th

Doug phoned again.

'Thanks so much for the posters,' he said.

'You're welcome. Were they ok?'

'They were perfect. I walked all around the streets this morning, and I stuck them to all the lampposts.'

'Great. I hope they do the trick.'

'Could you possibly send me some flyers, so that I can post them through people's doors?'

'But I... er... I...' I started. 'Yes, that's absolutely fine. How many would you like?'

'As many as you can do. 100?'

'No problem. I'll put them in the post to you today.'

On the way home from the Post Office I picked up some cookies to celebrate *National Cookie Day*, and we played Snakes and Ladders to celebrate *National Dice Day*. Do we know how to party, or what!.

December 5th

Bathtub Party Day encourages people to enjoy a long hot soak in a bath. I am not quite sure how a bathtub 'party' differs from 'having a bath', though. The creators of the holiday also encourage people to 'invite a friend'. No thanks! I chose to celebrate this holiday alone, but was interrupted after a few minutes by the phone downstairs.

'George, it's Doug,' shouted Rachel.

'Any news of Basil?' I asked, with a towel wrapped around me, shivering on the stairs.

'Nothing. I've been out and about looking for him all day, whistling and hoping he would appear, but there's been no sign of him. I delivered all of those flyers. Any chance you could print some more?'

'Ok,' I said.

'You're a star,' said Doug. 'It's awful not having you here to help look for him,'

'I know. It feels strange you having to do it all on your own.'

'You're not able to come back and help look for him with me, are you?'

I gave a slight laugh, assuming that he was joking, and then realised that he wasn't.

'I can't this week, I'm afraid, Doug. We'll be back in Northampton again in a few weeks and if he's not back then of course I will come and help look for him.'

'Ok. I understand.'

I was almost tempted to jump in the car and drive back to Northampton, but it seemed completely impractical, as there would not have been much I could do to help. Instead, I printed flyers until the printer ran out of ink, and the photo of Basil started to look like a faded grey cat instead of a black one. I then cycled to the Post Office to send Doug his third parcel in as many days.

I did feel dreadfully sorry for Doug and Chris. The cat was the focus of their lives, and every waking moment was now spent trying to get him back. On the two previous occasions on which he went missing, I was the one, spurred on by Doug, who put up the posters, delivered leaflets, and phoned the vets and animal shelters. I was now 250 miles away, but it was nice to be able to help as much as I could.

December 6th

They really do things properly in America. As well as *Thanksgiving* - the official start of the holiday season - they even have a dedicated day for switching on Christmas lights. *National Christmas Tree Lighting Day* takes place every year on the grassy area just south of the White House in Washington DC. Every year since 1923, they have had an official lighting of the tree. The tree itself has been replaced many times over the years.

We don't have an equivalent National Christmas Tree in the UK. In Washington this year, President Obama and his family switched on the lights. Our most famous Christmas lights are probably on London's Oxford Street, and this year they were switched on by pop star Jessie J. No disrespect to Jessie J, but she's not quite the same as President Obama. In previous years, when American presidents have flicked the switch to their National Christmas Tree, we have had S Club 7 and Peter Andre.

There was no delaying it any longer. Today would be the day that we put up our Christmas tree.

Because of Thanksgiving, I was trying to embrace Christmas this year. I'm usually a bit of a grouch around Christmas time. I enjoy the opportunity to get together with family, I like all the food and the drink, and I enjoy buying presents for people. But I'm a bit miserable when it comes to receiving presents. I've got so much 'stuff' already. Our lives are full of stuff and each Christmas our house becomes even fuller. Having three children makes this even more problematic. Although, Christmases have undoubtedly become more enjoyable since having children, as some of their infectious enthusiasm does of course rub off on me.

I have always hated shopping for Christmas trees, though. It is the second worst thing about Christmas (I will get to the first worst thing in a bit). Rachel always gets me to go and buy the tree as it's supposedly a 'man's job'. Every year I end up having a complete meltdown at the garden centre. Buying the Christmas tree is supposed to be a fun family activity; an exciting, symbolic act to signify the start of Christmas. Not in our house. To me, it is the first in many stressful and expensive duties over the festive period.

Rachel is particularly fussy about the type of tree that we have. It has to be big; big enough to look substantial in the sitting room, but narrow enough to fit into the small gap that we had allocated for it at our house in Northampton. It has to have branches evenly spaced from top to bottom; each branch must be of equal length. It has to be of the variety that does not shed its needles. Basically, she wants a real tree that looks and acts exactly like an artificial tree. I have suggested in the past that we just get an artificial one, but I didn't even get to finish the sentence before being adamantly told that it had to be a real one. I am also made to ask the garden centre staff to unwrap the already netted trees to check their suitability. But even after all of this, on one occasion a few years ago, I had to take a Christmas tree back to the shop from which I bought it, as Rachel insisted that I swap it for a taller, narrower, less droopy, greener one.

Our house in Devon has a good sized living room, with a high ceiling, so we could be a bit more adventurous with our tree this year. I decided to head off alone this year; choosing a tree with the children is a lovely idea in principle, but it actually makes the whole experience even more tedious.

I drove past a large hand painted sign simply saying 'CHRISTMAS TREES' recently, so thought this would be as good a place as any to get one. I followed the sign, which led me a mile to a roundabout, at which point another sign led me a further mile to another roundabout, and then another. These Christmas tree sellers had suckered me right in.

I eventually arrived at a caravan park, in the middle of nowhere, and followed another series of signs to a caravan at the far end, surrounded by Christmas trees. There were no other cars or customers, but a man soon emerged from the caravan. I told him my specifications, as prescribed by Rachel, and he found me a potential candidate. It was a fine specimen, which fulfilled the criteria, so he put it through the netting machine, I paid him his money, and I put the tree in the car boot.

Rachel told me it was the most perfect Christmas tree she had ever seen. Buying a tree this year was a strangely easy and almost enjoyable experience. It had been completely stress free, and effortless. I might even take the children with me next year. Could I finally be embracing Christmas?

All that festive cheer changed when it came to the Christmas tree lights. Putting up Christmas tree lights is, without a shadow of doubt, the number one worst thing about Christmas; probably the entire year. Even the most ardent Christmas enthusiast must still reach breaking point when they have to unravel the set of lights, that were so meticulously and carefully wound up the previous year, and which have somehow magically tied themselves into one big fuck off knot whilst in the attic.

Before untangling, I plugged them in to test them, and to my amazement they worked. I then spent the best part of an hour untangling them. Rachel and the kids like to decorate the tree, but apparently sorting out the lights is another man job that Rachel always delegates to me.

After wrapping the lights neatly around the tree, I then turned them on and discovered that the fucking things didn't work at all. I was past the point of no return. The children had already started to hang decorations onto the tree, and I wasn't going to take them off. I managed to find some spare bulbs in the bottom of the wardrobe, and after randomly swapping a couple of the bulbs over, half the lights started working again.

'I think that will have to do. Half is better than none,' I said to Rachel.

'I think it looks good. There's plenty of lights. Nobody will notice,' she said.

I posted something on Twitter saying that I had lost my annual battle with fairy lights again, and a friend of mine responded with:

'Life is too short not to buy new ones every year.'

I think I might have to adopt this philosophy in future.

'Your mum said we could borrow these lights, too,' said Rachel, holding up a ball of LED lights. 'I thought we could put them around the entire room.'

'Really? Won't that be a bit of a faff?'

'I don't mind doing it,' she said.

'Ok then. Go ahead.'

An hour later, Rachel was still standing on the back of the sofa trying to string the Christmas lights up.

'This ball of lights doesn't seem to be getting any smaller. Do you want to have a go?'

I raised my eyebrows at her.

'Plllleeeeeasssse,' she said.

'Ok, fine. Hand them over. Is it a man job too?'

'Yes, it is really. Thank you,' she said pathetically.

I completed another three full laps of the room with the fairy lights, yet the ball did not seem to have got any smaller. I then wrapped them up and down the two beams across the living room FOUR times, before eventually hiding the remainder of the lights behind the sofa.

'Where on earth did Mum get those lights from?' I asked.

'I think she said that your sister had used them at her wedding.'

'At her wedding? You mean the wedding that was in a bloody MARQUEE?'

'Yes, why?'

'It's no wonder these lights are so long. They were the ones used to line the inside of the marquee.'

'Oh, yes. I suppose that would explain it then.'

'You could have told me that crucial detail before I agreed to help.'

'Oops, sorry.'

'Well these lights will have to stay up all year round. I'm not taking them down again.'

We flicked the lights on and they genuinely provided more light than the actual main lights in the room. Whenever the fairy lights are on, we turn the other lights off, as the brightness can cause temporary blindness. They also default to a flickering '*disco*' setting, which means our living room is now a permanent rave. Oh how I love Christmas.

December 8th

'What is this strange item?' I asked Leo, as I held the TV remote control aloft.

'It's the TV remote-con-channel, of course,' laughed Leo.

Layla started calling remote controls 'remote con-channels' from a very early age, and despite initially trying to correct her, it stuck, and now all three children call it that. It does sort of make sense, as changing channels is its primary use. Rachel and I think it has a nice ring to it, so have adopted it, too.

'I have never seen a remote-con-channel before. Where I am from we do not have these,' I said.

All three children just looked at me like I was an idiot. This is quite a familiar look in our house.

'And what is this curious black object in my pocket?' I said, retrieving my phone. 'We do not have these where I am from.'

'Why are you being such a weirdo, Daddy? That's your phone,' said Layla.

'A phooone? What is this phone you speak of? We do not have those where I am from.'

'Mummy! Daddy has gone really weird. He's saying really odd things.'

'Weirder than normal?' said Rachel, walking into the room. 'Is that possible?'

'Who is this beautiful lady I see before me?' I said.

'That's Mummy. You call her Rachel. She's your wife, you wally.'

'Wow, I am a very lucky man. She is such a beauty. Where I am from we don't have such beautiful women.'

'Why is Daddy being silly?' asked Leo.

'I don't know, but I quite like this new Daddy, whoever he is. And where exactly are you from?' asked Rachel.

'I am from the year 1294. What year is it here?'

'It's 2013,' said Layla.

'Two thousand and thirteen. That means I'm over 700 years old.'

The kids all laughed.

'I knew you looked older than that old house we stayed at in Wales,' said Layla.

I gave her an evil look.

'What silly holiday are you celebrating today then?' asked Rachel.

'I don't know what you mean,' I said.

She left the room and returned a few seconds later with my diary.

'Ah... I see... today is *Pretend to be a Time Traveller Day*. Very good. Well, can you please pretend not to be a time traveller during Leo's birthday party this afternoon? There will be lots of parents here too, and we don't want you to scare them all off.'

Almost all of Leo's friends are girls. He does have a male friend - Stephen - but he got lost trying to find our house, so his party consisted of 10 girls and Leo. That's my boy.

December 9th

'What are you reading about?' asked Rachel between mouthfuls of cereal.

'Weary Willie,' I said.

'Weary willy? Shouldn't you go and see a Doctor about that?'

'Very funny. He was a clown character created by a circus performer called Emmett Leo Kelly in the early 1900s.'

'Why are you reading about a clown?'

'It's *Weary Willie Day* today.'

'What was special about Weary Willie compared to all other clowns?'

'Apparently he was quite unique in that he didn't have a white painted face. He wore makeup, but he was more of tramp character. He didn't do slapstick like other clowns, but people laughed at him because he was so tragic.'

'Poor Weary Willie. What did he do that was so tragic?'

'It says that part of his act would be to come on and clear up after each of the circus performers. He would spend ages trying to sweep up the pool of light on the floor made by the spotlight.'

'I like the sound of him. How are you going to celebrate?'

'I know!' shouted Layla, who had been eavesdropping from the other end of the table.

'How?' I asked.

'We're going to paint your face to look like a clown.'

'But it's only 8am. And it's Monday.'

'So? Mummy, where are the face-paints?'

'I'll just go and get them for you. That sounds like a great idea.'

As Monday mornings go, having your face painted first thing was actually a pretty great start to the week.

'Happy *Weary Willie Day*, Daddy,' they said.

December 10th

Layla's wobbly tooth had still not fallen out. Every day for months, she has been convinced that today would be the day her first tooth would finally fall out. In the past few days, I had started to believe her. She asked me to pull it out for her to end her misery, but I wimped out and told her it would be more exciting if it fell out on its own.

We were eating dinner together and Layla suddenly gasped and started frantically spitting out a mouthful of her food.

'What's the matter?' asked Rachel. 'Are you ok?'

'My tooth!' spluttered Layla through her food. 'My tooth has fallen out.'

She looked up to reveal a gap where her tooth had been, which is what tends to happen after a tooth falls out.

'Yey, finally! How exciting!' I said. 'Where is it?'

'I don't know,' she said, prodding at the chewed up sausage and mash on her plate.

'It must be in there somewhere,' said Rachel, beginning a thorough forensic investigation of the food matter.

'Did you swallow it?' I asked.

'I don't know. I tried to spit it out but I think I did swallow something.'

I tried not to laugh.

'So you swallowed your tooth and spat out your food?' I said.

'I'm sorry. I didn't mean to.'

'Don't worry, darling. It doesn't matter,' said Rachel.

'Yes it does. Now the Tooth Fairy won't come and visit me and I won't get any money.'

'I'm sure you will,' I said, looking at Rachel for confirmation.

'Of course you will,' she said.

'But how will the Tooth Fairy know that my tooth has fallen out if there's no tooth?'

'You could write her a note to explain what happened?' I said. 'I'm sure she would understand.'

'That's a good idea,' said Rachel. 'Why don't you write her a letter when you've finished your dinner?'

'What are we going to do about the tooth?' asked Rachel, once Layla was in the other room.

'What do you mean what are we going to do?'

'I mean, we'll have to try and retrieve it, won't we?'

'Retrieve it? No we won't. That tooth is GONE.'

'Whatever goes in must come out.'

'Yes, but that doesn't mean that we need to see it again.'

'But I've got that special '*My First Tooth*' pot that I wanted to keep all of the kids' first teeth in.'

'Well you can just put her second tooth in it when that falls out. They all look the same anyway.'

'But I will always know that it wasn't her first tooth.'

'What are you suggesting?'

'I think you need to do the honourable thing and conduct a search and recovery operation once the time comes.'

'You want me to search through Layla's poo?'

'It's what a good father should do.'

'Why me? You're the one who wants it back so desperately.'

'But it's a man's job.'

'Since when has searching through poo been a man's job?'

'Since today.'

'That's convenient.'

'Did you know that according to your diary it's *Jane Addams Day* today?' she asked.

'No. Who is Jane Addams?'

'She was an American pioneer, philosopher and suffragette.'

'And? What's that got to do with me searching through poo?'

'She fought for women to have equal rights to men.'

'Well I'm all for equality. I think it's time that women had equal rights to search poo as men. It should no longer be a man's job.'

'That's very noble of you, but I think you need to take control of this situation. Those suffragettes gave their lives to give women the chance to vote. So I'm voting for you to do it. Do it for me. Do it for Layla. Do it for Jane Addams and the suffragettes. Do it for the tooth.'

'You talk so much crap. Literally. Fine, I'll do it then.'

'Thank you. I knew you would.'

'Don't think that I'm happy about this. How long will I have to wait?'

'Poo watch begins now.'

December 11th

I decided to nip out for a quick run before the kids went to school. When I returned, Rachel was standing in the kitchen with her eyebrows raised at me disapprovingly. I noticed she was wearing a pair of rubber gloves.

'What the matter?' I asked.

'You were supposed to be on poo watch. It came.'

'The tooth? You got the tooth back?'

'No, but not through lack of trying. You weren't here so I had to take matters into my own hands.'

'That's an interesting choice of words.'

'Some father you are,' she said, peeling off the gloves and dropping them in the bin.

'Oh well, maybe next time,' I said.

'You'd better be ready for it next time. This is not over.'

After picking up Layla from school, I dropped her at home and then had to go to the supermarket to get some noodles for tonight's dinner. I got home again to find Rachel walking down the stairs, with another accusing look on her face, and another pair of rubber gloves on her hands.

'Oh no, I missed it again, did I? What a shame.'

'Are you doing this on purpose?'

'Of course not! I really want to be there for this historic occasion. I'm really gutted to have missed the opportunity again. Did you find it?'

'No. So don't worry, your opportunity will come.'

'No it won't,' interrupted Layla from upstairs. 'I don't want that tooth back. Please forget about it.'

'But it's your very first tooth, darling,' said Rachel.

'I don't care. I've got plenty more. They are all the same.'

'Are you sure?'

Layla stood at the top of the stairs sobbing.

'Yes, I'm sure. Please stop,' said Layla. 'I don't like you searching through my poo. It's really embarrassing. The tooth fairy gave me my money. Why would I need my silly tooth back now? Especially as it will be really gross and smelly.'

'Yes, Rachel. Why WOULD anyone want to get that gross and smelly tooth back?' I said.

'Ok, darling. Let's just forget about it then,' said Rachel, casting me an evil glare as I grinned smugly.

254

Today was *Noodle Ring Day*. I assumed that a noodle ring was just what Americans call spaghetti hoops, and I was secretly excited about having spaghetti hoops on toast for dinner. It turns out a Noodle Ring is an actual thing. Apparently once quite popular in the middle of the 19th century, it involves baking noodles and eggs with cheese in a ring mould, and then filling the centre with something like tuna. I didn't have a ring mould, so baked it in a cake tin, and then scooped out the middle. It looked rank but tasted surprisingly good.

December 13th

I almost celebrated *Violin Day* with the sound of violins played at my own funeral. Today was probably the closest I have ever come to dying. I was convinced it was the end. I didn't see my life flash before my eyes, but I did feel a wave of emotion that signified that was it. My time was up. How did it happen, you ask? A near-miss in a car? An accident on my bike? Slipping on a rock along the coastal path?

Not quite.

I was brushing my teeth.

I'm not entirely sure how it happened. I was brushing my teeth as normal, and at the point at which my mouth was full of toothpaste, I involuntarily coughed and breathed in at the same time, if that's even physically possible. Anyway, the contents of my mouth, which was an extra-minty, extreme deep-clean, added fluoride, cavity protection, whitest teeth ever, sensitive plus toothpaste, was instantly transported from inside my mouth into my airway.

I couldn't breathe.

It felt as if my lungs had filled with foam that had expanded to fill every inch of empty space. I gasped for air, but there was no route through for the air to travel. I tried to cough, but there was nothing in my lungs to eject the toothpaste. I tried to hit myself on the back. I even attempted to give myself the Heimlich manoeuvre, which it turns out is not physically possible.

I stared at myself in the mirror. Was this it? Was this the way I was going to die? Of all the ways to go, a bizarre tooth brushing accident would be a pretty lame end. I looked at my helpless reflection in the mirror, and could already see the colour had drained from my face.

I couldn't shout for help. I couldn't scream. Rachel was downstairs and would not be able to hear me even if I could. I was going to die alone, on the bathroom floor, in a pool of my own toothpaste.

I rushed from the bathroom and descended the stairs, four steps at a time. You take risks like that, I discovered, when your life depends on it. I burst into the sitting room to find Rachel on the sofa, just at the instant I felt a tiny gap clear in my throat, enough for a small hiss of air to seep into my lungs. Again I tried to force myself to cough and I spluttered up a mouthful of foam onto the carpet in front of Rachel.

'Oh my God. Are you alright?' she said, jumping to her feet.

'Huuuuhhheeeeerrrr,' I gasped, trying to suck another mouthful of air into my lungs, bent double in the middle of the sitting room, still clutching my toothbrush.

'What happened?' she said, rushing over and giving my back a pat.

'Tooooth paaaaaste,' I said, pointing to my throat as I continued to wheeze.

Eventually I was able to clear my throat enough to speak properly, but even after drinking lots of water, my throat and my airway continued to burn, as though I had gargled a cocktail of battery acid and broken glass. The burning sensation remained for several hours. I assume it was a combination of the coughing, and the mint from the toothpaste making contact with a part of the body not expected to deal with such a substance.

'That was nasty,' said Rachel. 'Poor you.'

'I honestly thought I was going to die.'

'Well I'm glad you didn't.'

'Me too. If I had died, at least I would have been remembered by having the cleanest teeth and the mintiest fresh breath.'

'Yes, I suppose that's true.'

It really did open my eyes to the fragility of life and the dangers of tooth brushing.

Strangely, yesterday was *National 12-Hour Fresh Breath Day*. Although I did obviously brush my teeth yesterday, I didn't 'celebrate' the holiday with any fanfare. Perhaps this was toothpaste's way of wreaking revenge.

December 15th

'Did you have fun at swimming?' I asked Kitty, when she walked into my study late afternoon.

She looked at me quizzically.

'We didn't go swimming.'

'I thought you all went swimming this morning?'

'No. Not this day. We went swimming on other day. Not this day.'

'Are you sure? Mummy said you were going today.'

'We did go swimming but not this day. On other day.'

'Oh, ok then,' I said.

I checked with Rachel and they had indeed been swimming in the morning. But since then, they had also been to the cafe, to the supermarket, and to see some friends for the afternoon. Kitty had had a short nap in the car, and seemed unable to grasp the concept that all of these events could possibly have taken place within the same day.

It got me thinking. It was a similar philosophy that this holiday challenge is based on. Children have little concept of time because their days are so full of activity and new experiences. The more you do, the more you can slow time down.

It also made me think about the significance of her nap after lunch, too. Perhaps her mind found it hard to differentiate this sleep with her night-time sleep, and waking from her nap was, in a sense, beginning a new day.

Perhaps the Spanish are onto something with their siestas. Far from wasting time by sleeping, they are actually doubling the number of days in a year, and the number of days in their life. I suggested the idea of incorporating a mid-afternoon nap into my daily routine to Rachel, and she just glared at me and then laughed assuming I was joking.

I laughed too in order to avoid any further repercussions.

December 16th

All food tastes good covered in chocolate, right? Wrong.

It was *Chocolate Covered Anything Day*, so we decided to put it to the test. I asked Layla, Leo, and Kitty what they would like to cover in chocolate.

'Batfink,' said Leo.

'The car,' said Layla.

'Mummy,' said Kitty.

'Well, although that would be quite funny, I don't think Batfink or Mummy would like it, and the car might be difficult to drive if it was covered in chocolate.'

'Ooooh, you asked us what we wanted to cover in chocolate,' argued Leo.

'I know I did, sorry. I meant to ask, what FOOD would you like to cover in chocolate? Today is *Chocolate Covered Anything Day*, so we can cover your favourite foods in chocolate to make them taste EVEN better.'

'Popcorn!' shouted Layla.

'Ok, we could do that. Kitty? What about you? What's your favourite food?'

'Cucumber.'

'Cucumber? Err... '

'And Ketchup,' she added.

'Right, ok. We could try that.'

'Leo? What about you? What food would you like us to cover in chocolate?'

'Pizza.'

'Anything else? Maybe grapes or strawberries or something?'

'No. Pizza is my favourite food. I want it covered in chocolate, please.'

'Ok. Let's do it.'

Chocolate covered popcorn was great, as you would expect. Cucumber and pizza, not so much.

December 18th

I had not had a mobile phone signal since moving to our house in August. I am tied into a contract for another year before I can switch networks. To get a signal, I have to climb a hill in a nearby field, and stand amongst the cows and the cowpats with my arm stretched towards the sky. I haven't missed having a phone signal. Almost all of my work enquiries come via email, and we have a landline too, so it's not essential.

I used to get an awful lot of business sales calls anyway, which I certainly don't miss. *Was I interested in selling my business? Was I set up to take credit card payments and would my company benefit if I was? Did I want to change the energy supplier for my business? Have I considered changing suppliers for my wedding albums? Can I speak to the Marketing Manager?*

The answer was always no, no, no. I am usually too courteous with them, though, and will always listen to what they have to say, and then politely tell them that I'm not interested at the moment, but '*sure, please do call me back in three months time*', when I still won't be interested, but we can go through all of it again.

Having no phone signal obviously brought a halt to these calls. However, when I ventured out to places that did have coverage, my phone had a habit of ringing within seconds with a sales call. Either these companies were freakishly lucky, or, more likely, they had automated systems in place that keep trying phone numbers until they get a ringtone on the other end.

It was *Answer the Telephone Like Buddy the Elf Day*. The Christmas movie Elf, starring Will Ferrell, is undoubtedly one of the greatest Christmas films of ever. I have watched it countless times, and it never fails to make me laugh.

In the film, Buddy answers the phone in his father's New York office with the line: '*Buddy the Elf, what's your favourite colour?*' Buddy's father then snatches the phone from Buddy but the caller has already hung up.

I went into town and sure enough my phone rang twice in the space of five minutes. Both times I answered it with '*Buddy the Elf, what's your favourite colour?*' Both times the caller hung up immediately.

I planned to answer all sales calls like that from then on. Actually, I can't be sure that both of those were sales calls. Oh well.

December 19th

The phone rang at 3:24am this morning. I can remember the exact time because I sat bolt upright in bed the second it sounded, and stared at the alarm clock as a horrendous feeling of sickness gripped me. Rachel sat up too and just stared at the phone for a couple of seconds.

The only time the phone rings at that time of the night is if someone is calling with terrible news.

I climbed out of bed and walked apprehensively to the phone, my heart pounding.

'Hello,' I said anxiously.

Before the caller even had a chance to speak I could hear a familiar noise in the background. It was the loud, needy, and unmistakable meow of Father Dougal.

'George? Guess who's back?' said Doug.

'Basil!' I shouted. 'Where did you find him?'

'He just came running through the cat flap about five minutes ago. It's a miracle.'

'He found his own way home? That's amazing. Any idea where he had been?'

'No idea. What a little tinker, eh?'

'Well, that's brilliant news, Doug. I'm so pleased you've got him back. Does he look ok?'

'He's looking a bit skinny but he seems healthy enough. He hasn't stopped meowing since he came in, and he's been sprinting around all over the house like a mad thing.'

'I can hear him. He sounds like he's very pleased to be home. It's so good that he's back before Christmas, too.'

'Oh, it is, George. This is the best Christmas present ever. It has been such an awful few weeks for us. I don't think Chris and I will be going back to sleep tonight after this.'

'By the sound of things, I don't think Basil would let you anyway. Rachel and I are both delighted. Thanks for letting us know and we're looking forward to seeing you when we're back in Northampton next week.'

'Looking forward to it. Take care, kiddo.'

December 20th

Today was *Go Carolling Day* so we all went to a Christmas service and carol concert at our small local church that sits at the top of a hill. I didn't really enjoy being dragged along to carol concerts as a child, but they did come to signify Christmas time, so Rachel and I thought it would be good to get the children into the habit of going to church, even if only once a year.

We got there a few minutes before it was due to start, but the church was already full, so the vicar directed us down to sit in the pews usually used by the choir. We were facing the rest of the congregation, and the vicar's pulpit was directly behind us, so she was conducting her sermon directly into our ears.

Kitty had a bad cold, and was not feeling very well. She was quite fidgety and annoying, so Rachel decided to take her out after a couple of minutes. Take her out of the church, that is; not a brutal wrestling manoeuvre.

'Can we go too?' asked Leo.

'No. You, me and Layla will stay for the whole thing, I'm afraid,' I whispered. 'We'll meet Mummy in the car afterwards.'

After bluffing my way through several hymns that I didn't recognise, a lady from the parish then stood up to do a reading.

Lots of people in the congregation appeared to be smiling at me, and I then noticed that Leo had leaned his head against the pew end and was fast asleep. I smiled back to them, secretly relieved, as a sleeping Leo was less problematic than an awake Leo.

He then started to snore.

Very, very loudly.

He has always been a noisy sleeper, ever since he was born, and often keeps the other two awake with his snoring. There were a few sniggers from the elderly church-goers, so I picked him up and sat him on my lap, and the adjustment seemed to quieten him down.

It was then time for the vicar to do her sermon. Leo started snoring heavily again, so I flipped him around, so that his head was on my shoulder, hoping my neck would muffle the noise. The deeper into sleep he went, the louder the snoring got.

The vicar then asked everyone to pause in prayer for a minute, to remember those from the parish that had passed away during the last year.

Being in the middle of nowhere, there was no sound of traffic, no murmur of a distant radio, no machinery; just complete and utter silence. Apart from Leo, who snored like a beast throughout.

I did my best to readjust him, but I didn't want to draw further attention to it, so just looked at my feet and prayed to God like everyone else. It was the longest minute of my life.

Thankfully, Layla was as good as gold throughout, and at the end of the service I apologised profusely to the vicar, who wasn't bothered in the slightest. She told me that she often feels like having a nap in church, too.

December 21st

Humbug Day encourages people to vent their Christmas frustrations four days before Christmas, so their mind and body can be free of stress for the holidays.

December 21st is usually the date on which I start panicking about Christmas; I realise I haven't bought all (any) of my presents yet and I don't feel prepared in the slightest. This year was different. This year I genuinely felt ready. I had bought all of my presents, we had bought most of the food, the house was relatively tidy, and the beds were already prepared for our guests.

Making the decision to not publish *Every Day Is a Holiday* before Christmas was a huge weight off my shoulders, and the whole build up to Christmas had been remarkably easy. My final wedding of the year had been in early December and I was almost up-to-date with my other work.

We have a stupid annoying doorbell with 36 different melodies to choose from. They are activated by pressing a large button on the receiver, plugged into a socket in our kitchen. The children press the button all of the goddamn time, which not only makes me rush to the door to answer it, but it changes the melody so that I don't recognise the sound of the doorbell the next time it chimes. But today, full of Christmas cheer, I didn't mind about our stupid annoying doorbell. In fact, I deliberately changed the melody to '*We Wish You a Merry Christmas.*' I would not be taking part in *Humbug Day* this year.

December 23rd

On December 18th, 1997, an episode of Seinfeld aired that revealed the holiday of *Festivus*. *Festivus* was a holiday celebrated by the family of Seinfeld writer Dan O'Keefe, and he introduced it to the world through the much-loved *Seinfeld* character George Costanza.

Festivus is an alternative celebration to Christmas. It is '*a Festivus for the rest of us*,' and the day has several established traditions that are now observed by many who have adopted *Festivus* as their own.

This year, we celebrated *Festivus* too.

The focal point of the *Festivus* holiday is an unadorned aluminium pole, used in contrast to the materialism of modern day Christmas trees. A simple meal then begins (some suggest meatloaf or spaghetti, as depicted in the *Seinfeld* episode, but the rules aren't too strict). No alcohol is served. Then follows the '*airing of grievances*,' during which the guests are gathered together, and you are encouraged to tell your family members the ways in which they have disappointed you during the year.

'That sounds fun,' said Rachel. 'Shall I go first?'

'Ok then. Let's get it over and done with. Is this going to take all night?'

'Firstly, you always dump your clothes on the bedroom floor, instead of putting them away.'

'But that's because it's always dark when I come to be..'

'Quiet! I haven't finished,' she interrupted. 'Secondly, your study is always ridiculously messy.'

'But...'

'I haven't finished. Thirdly, you never rinse the shower tray or the bath when you've washed off, after going to the beach. You just leave all the sand in there and it's really gross.'

'Is that everything? Ok, I get it. I'm a bit messy. Fair enough.'

'Yes, that's all I can think of at the moment. What about your grievances?'

'Ok, here goes. You buy too many bags-for-life.'

'But when I get to the...'

'Shhh, be quiet. It's my turn. You put too much water in the kettle and boil it far too many times, and never even make tea.'

'Ok.'

'And you never turn lights off when you leave the room.'

'Is that everything?'

'Yes, I think so. Oh, and you've got too many coats.'

'Done?'

'Done. I feel better now.'

'Me too. That was actually good fun.'

'I was expecting a lot worse, to be fair.'

'Both lists were pretty trivial really,' said Rachel. 'So you're too messy and I'm a bit rubbish with kettles, lights and bags.'

'And coats,' I added.

'Well I think you and I are doing ok,' she said giving me a kiss. 'Happy Festivus.'

'Happy Festivus to you, too.'

'So, is *Festivus* over for the year?'

'No. Now it is time for the *Feats of Strength*.'

'What is that?'

'According to Frank - that's George Costanza'a dad - '*Festivus is not over until the head of the household is wrestled to the floor and pinned*.'

'Who is the head of the household?'

'Duh! That will be me, of course,' I said.

'Really? I always assumed it was me.'

'I know you did, but this is my game, so I am head of the household. Even if only for today.'

'Fine.'

I managed to fend Rachel off successfully for a while, and it felt like *Festivus* would never end. But then she called for reinforcements who came armed with pillows, a skipping rope and a wooden sword. A massive whack in the bollocks from

266

Leo's sword followed, and I was pinned to the floor within seconds. *Festivus* was over.

December 24th

We used to divide our time at Christmas between my parents and Rachel's parents. They only lived about three miles from each other in Northampton, so it was fairly easy to spend an equal amount of time with both families. This year, we were hosting Christmas at our house, and both sets of parents were coming to us.

Rachel's mum and dad arrived mid-afternoon on Christmas Eve, and within an hour I was already making up the second batch of mulled wine. I made eggnog, too, for the very first time. Eggnog is one of those things that everyone in the UK has heard of, but most have probably never tried. Today was *Eggnog Day*, and not only did I try it for the first time, but I realised what I had been missing out on for the past 35 years. Why do we only drink these two delicious drinks at Christmas? I'm going to start drinking eggnog and mulled wine year-round.

December 25th

On each birthday that Layla, Leo and Kitty have celebrated, I have taken a photograph of them sitting with a piece of paper with their age written on it. We did it spontaneously for Layla's first birthday and decided to continue for every birthday since. It has been fun to keep a visual record of them growing older over the years. I hope to carry it on for as long as I can, although, during their teenage years - when they are way too cool to spend their birthdays with their boring old parents - I will have to encourage them to send me a selfie instead.

In June this year, for the first time, we forgot to take Layla's photograph during the day of her birthday. We remembered late in the evening, once she was fast asleep. We debated waking her, but instead lay a number six beside her, and took a photo of her asleep on her bed, surrounded by her Barbies (this was before the massacre).

The photos had all accumulated on my computer over the years and Rachel and I often talked about getting them printed, but had never got around to it. For part of Rachel's Christmas present this year, I bought 12 small frames from local charity shops - so that they each looked unique - and framed these photographs. We hung them on the wall and we can add to the rows as they grow up.

It takes a brave or foolish person to create another holiday on December 25th. However, *Christmas Day* is also *A'phabet Day*, or *No 'L' Day*. The day is a poor pun on the word Noel, and people are encouraged to speak, write, and text during the day without using the letter L.

It's a fairly stupid idea, to be honest, and one that I am sure is not even observed by the person who created it. I did debate writing up today's entry without using the letter L, just to show willing. You will be relieved to hear I decided against it. It would have been immensely irritating for you to read, and a real bastard for my computer's spell check. But if you really want to get into the spirit of this holiday, feel free to omit the Ls when reading the remainder of this section.

There was something special this Christmas about being at our own house for a change, and not having to get in the car and drive somewhere. The children were able to enjoy their presents once opened, and we didn't have to watch the clock to get ready for our next engagement. Despite having to cook a Christmas dinner for nine people, *Christmas Day* felt more relaxing than ever. As neither of us had to drive anywhere, it meant that both Rachel and I could drink, too, which was definitely a bonus.

I ate and drank far too much, but fortunately did not embarrass myself this time with any waffle eating contests or MC Hammer dance-offs.

December 27th

The days between Christmas and New Year are strange sort of nothing days. Those who have to go back to work, do so half-heartedly, because work colleagues are often still on annual leave. Those who book the time off, tend to exist in a drunken chocolate-induced coma, as the days between Christmas and New Year merge into one. Time is spent either moving between various relatives' houses or sitting at home in front of continuous Christmas specials on the television.

There are very few holidays scheduled for these days, presumably because the Christmas period is already filled with celebrations; or perhaps, more likely, because the creators themselves are too busy comatose on the sofa to even consider celebrating something else.

We all had a nice walk on the beach on *Boxing Day* and I bottled out of going for my traditional *Boxing Day* sea swim (I had never been for a *Boxing Day* sea swim, but had wanted to turn it into a tradition). We then went home, ate turkey sandwiches and slipped into our food comas for the rest of the evening.

The following morning, both sets of parents headed back to Northampton, and we packed the car and drove up there in the afternoon to spend a few days catching up with friends and family.

December 28th

A vast number of aunts, uncles, cousins, children and dogs, descended on my parents' house for our annual Christmas gathering. We used to all buy presents for each other, but we jointly realised that, as the family was so big and ever-increasing, it was unnecessary, and completely impractical. For the last six years, we have operated a Secret Santa gift system, so we only have to buy a single gift for a nominated member of the extended family. It has made things so much simpler and it always works really well.

Today was *Card Playing Day*, and after the extended family departed, Rachel and I sat down for a game of Cribbage against my mum and dad.

'THEY say you should NEVER lead with a seven or an eight,' said Dad, predictably, as I boldly placed down the Seven of Clubs.

'According to Hoyle, you should ALWAYS lead with a seven,' I said.

270

Rachel and I lost the game spectacularly, but I felt a sense of victory at no longer being dictated to by 'they'.

December 29th

Tick Tock Day is strategically placed a few days before the end of the year. The day was created to encourage people to think about whether they have achieved everything they set out to at the start of the year. If not, then there is still time to cram in a few more things before the year is out.

My year had been crammed fuller than ever, but I still had a few days of the year remaining, and a few things still to do. Tick tock.

After another Christmas 'do' - this time with Rachel's extended family - we went to visit Rachel's Granddad, who was unfortunately unwell in hospital, and then on to see Doug and Chris.

Basil was on fine form, and looked to be back to his usual fat and loud self. The new neighbours had announced to Doug and Chris that they were expecting their first baby. Doug and Chris were both delighted with the news, and it was comforting to think that we had almost gone full circle, with a new family beginning in the house where we began ours.

'Have a very Happy New Year, both of you,' I said, as we got ready to leave.

'Thank you, we will,' said Doug. 'God bless all of you. Thanks ever so much for coming to visit and make sure you come and see us again soon.'

'We will. Oh yes, I keep forgetting to tell you, I've nearly finished writing my second book.'

'How exciting. What's it about? Is it another bike ride like your last one?'

'This one is very different. It's a bit hard to explain. You feature in it, though.'

'Me?'

'Yes, you and Chris are both in it. And Basil features quite regularly, too.'

'Oh, how tremendous. Did you hear that, Chris, love? We are in a book. We're going to be famous!'

'I will send you a copy in the New Year as soon as it's out.'

'Fantastic. I can't wait. Well done, kiddo.'

As we were walking back to the car we heard a car horn. I looked up to see a silver BMW slowing down as it neared us. The window was wound down and a familiar face was leaning out.

It was Ian Stewart - my Facebook un-friend.

Unbe-fucking-lievable.

'Merry Christmas, George. Did you have a good one?'

'Very good thanks, Ian. How about you?'

'Brilliant. Listen, give me a shout next time you're up and we'll meet up for that beer, yeah?'

'Definitely, Ian. That sounds great,' I said.

I received another Facebook friend request from Ian later that evening accompanied by a message.

'Hi George. Facebook seems to have unfriended us by mistake again. Ian'

I clicked *accept*. We were friends again. This time it would be for good.

December 30th

After an enjoyable few days in Northampton, it was time to load the car and head back down to Devon. We stopped for lunch at McDonald's on the way home. There was one last thing I wanted to achieve before the year was out.

'What can I get you, Sir?' asked James, the young man behind the counter. He had four stars on his name badge, so I knew he was an experienced member of staff.

'Hello. Could I have three Fish Finger Happy Meals please - all with orange juice - a Quarter Pounder with Cheese Meal with a Coke. And then a Mc... er... '

I looked both ways.

I was alone at the counter.

'And a McGangBang, please. With a fries and a Coke.'

'Anything else, Sir?' he asked, with only a faint glimmer of a smile.

Perhaps he hadn't heard me.

'Er, no, that's everything thanks.'

A few minutes later he put a tray on the counter in front of me, stacked it high with three Happy Meals and Rachel's meal. He then added an extra item in a brown McDonald's bag.

'There you go, Sir. The McGangBang is in this bag,' he whispered, tapping the bag gently and giving me a knowing wink. 'Enjoy your meal!'

'Thank you. I will,' I said, as I walked away with a spring in my step, feeling like the champion of the world.

Today was *Falling Needles Family Fest Day*, a day when the family are encouraged to gather together and sit and watch the needles fall from the Christmas tree. The Christmas tree that I had bought was still looking particularly healthy and was

273

dropping very few needles. We sat on the sofa and watched it for a few seconds anyway, before getting bored and watching *Elf* again instead.

It had been lovely having people to stay, and great fun catching up with friends and family back in Northampton, but there was something equally wonderful about sitting on the sofa, with no guests, and no further commitments, after an exhausting but unforgettable Christmas.

December 31st

Moving to Devon had worked out even better than we hoped. Great Britain had experienced its wettest winter on record, and it honestly felt like it has rained non-stop since we moved. Yet we had somehow loved every minute of it. Imagine how much fun it would be when the sun came out.

Would we be living in Devon had it not been for this holiday challenge? I honestly don't know. But I do know for certain that it would not have happened the way it has, and I wouldn't change any of it if I could.

The year had felt longer than any year I have ever known. This is a good thing. By filling my days with new experiences, my concept of time has slowed down. Without the holiday celebrations, next year will undoubtedly feel slightly empty in comparison. But I know that some of the state-of-mind associated with this challenge will stay with me. I am more open to trying new things than I ever was. I say yes more. I appreciate my family and friends more than ever. I try to seize the day (even Mondays). I am aware of time slipping by and I want to enjoy every moment that I'm on this earth, however long that might be. I want to embrace each day and I will make the most of the boring days too, and fill the time surrounding them with things I love. This may be the end of the holiday challenge, but it is not the end of the adventure. This is just the beginning.

I had not found the hidden lever to unlock the secret of the mirror maze, but I had found MY hidden lever that unlocks my own personal happiness. Actually, reading that back, it sounds like a euphemism about my penis. I should probably delete that bit.

We were invited to the pub with a group of friends for a *New Year's Eve* party, but Rachel and I decided to stay home. This wasn't me neglecting to celebrate the final holiday of the year; it was me choosing to see in the New Year with my family instead. Also, to be perfectly honest, we couldn't get a babysitter.

I tucked the children into bed and gave them each a kiss.
'See you next year,' I said.
'What do you mean? Where are you going, Daddy?' asked Leo.
'Yeah, Daddy,' said Kitty. 'Where are you going?'
'He's just being silly,' said Layla.
'Are you just being silly?' said Leo.
'Yes, I was. Sorry. It was just a little joke. A new year starts tomorrow. I'm not going anywhere. Sleep well, all of you.'

Rachel and I spent the evening on the sofa with a delicious dinner and a bottle (or three) of wine. As we watched the TV coverage of the fireworks over London's South Bank, and Big Ben sounded out the end of the year, I realised there was no place I would rather be.

I still have lots of work in Northampton next year so will continue to drive up there regularly. There is no doubt that each journey back has got harder, and felt longer than the one before it. My plan was always to rebuild my photography career once we were settled in Devon, but for various reasons - other than my single Devon wedding - this hasn't happened.

I realised recently that I don't want to be a photographer anymore. It has been an immensely enjoyable job that I feel very privileged to have done, but my heart is no longer in it. I became a photographer because photography was my passion, and I wanted to turn it into a career. I have now found a greater passion.

When I started this challenge at the beginning of January, it was all about new experiences and trying new things. I am not going to pretend that I didn't want to write a book about it, but that was never my sole intention. What I didn't expect was how much I would enjoy the writing. Yes, the holidays themselves were fun, but it was writing about them that gave me a buzz I have never before experienced. What I have learned most during the year is how I don't want this to end. I have lots of exciting ideas for future books, but it has always been difficult to take the writing seriously and juggle a career at the same time.

Today, *New Year's Eve* - the final day of the year - is *Make Up Your Mind Day*, and for the last few weeks I have been considering closing the shutter on my photography career (bad pun intended). Today - *Make Up Your Mind Day* - I have finally made up my mind. Next year will be my last as a photographer.

I am going to become an author.

Author's Note

Thank you so much for sharing this strange year with me. I would be extremely grateful if you would consider leaving a short review on Amazon or Goodreads (it only needs to be a few words). Self-published authors rely almost exclusively on your reviews and recommendations to friends and family, so any way in which you can help spread the word would be massively appreciated. Thank you!

All of the photographs in this book are available to view in high-resolution on Facebook.
www.facebook.com/georgemahood

You can also follow me on Instagram and Twitter:
@georgemahood

I have a website, but there is not much to see there.
If you sign up to the newsletter you will be the first to hear about any new releases.
www.georgemahood.com

I have written many other books. They can be read in any order and are all available in paperback, audiobook and ebook. Please take a look…

Also by George Mahood

Every Day Is a Holiday:
The hilarious true story of one dad's attempt to celebrate the weird and wonderful calendar days

Free Country:
A Penniless Adventure the Length of Britain

Not Tonight, Josephine:
A Road Trip Through Small-Town America

Travels with Rachel:
In Search of South America

Operation Ironman:
One Man's Four Month Journey from Hospital Bed to Ironman Triathlon

Did Not Finish:
Misadventures in Running, Cycling and Swimming

The Self-Help Bible:
All the Answers for a Happier, Healthier Life

How Not to Get Married:
A no-nonsense guide to weddings, from a photographer who has seen it ALL

FREE COUNTRY:
A Penniless Adventure the Length of Britain

The plan is simple. George and Ben have three weeks to cycle 1000 miles from the bottom of England to the top of Scotland. There is just one small problem... they have no bikes, no clothes, no food and no money. Setting off in just a pair of Union Jack boxer shorts, they attempt to rely on the generosity of the British public for everything from food to accommodation, clothes to shoes, and bikes to beer.

During the most hilarious adventure, George and Ben encounter some of Great Britain's most eccentric and extraordinary characters and find themselves in the most ridiculous situations. Free Country is guaranteed to make you laugh (you may even shed a tear). It will restore your faith in humanity and leave you with a big smile on your face and a warm feeling inside.

NOT TONIGHT, JOSEPHINE:
A Road Trip Through Small-Town America

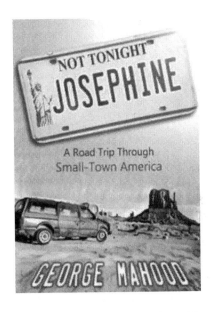

Two Brits, George and Mark, set off from New York City to explore the back roads of America. In this calamity-ridden travel tale, George sets out in true clichéd fashion to discover the real America.

Throw in plenty of run-ins with the police, rapidly dwindling finances and Josephine – the worst car in the world - and you have all the ingredients for a classic American road trip. Will George and Mark make it all the way to California?

And then there is Rachel, George's girlfriend, left back in England. Would travelling to the United States without her turn out to be the stupidest decision he had ever made?

OPERATION IRONMAN:
One Man's Four Month Journey from Hospital Bed to Ironman Triathlon

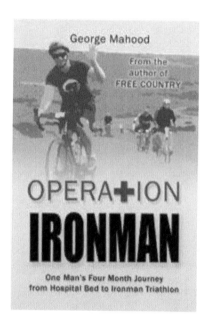

Operation Ironman follows George Mahood's inspiring and entertaining journey from a hospital bed to an Ironman triathlon. After major surgery to remove a spinal cord tumour, George set himself the ultimate challenge –

a 2.4 mile swim,

a 112 mile bike ride,

and a 26.2 mile run,

all to be completed within 16 hours.

He couldn't swim more than a length of front crawl, he had never ridden a proper road bike, and he had not run further than 10k in 18 months.

He had four months to prepare.

Could he do it?

THE SELF-HELP BIBLE:
All the Answers for a Happier, Healthier Life

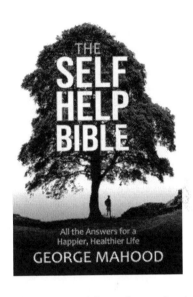

George Mahood is not a philosopher, scientist, theologian or psychologist. He is just a fairly average guy who feels like he could be happier and healthier.

He began reading self-help books with the hope of improving his life, but was left frustrated and underwhelmed by a lot of what he read. So, he decided to write his own.

You should not be expected to read all the books George did to try to better your own life. He did all the reading for you. And he has shared with you what he learned.

This is the only self-help book you will ever need!

In his usual humorous, down-to-earth style, George covers all aspects of self-improvement and personal development. From mindfulness to mindset, food to fear of failure, habits to health, exercise to education, mental health to morning routines, self-love to sleep, The Self-Help Bible has it all.

TRAVELS WITH RACHEL:
In Search of South America

Knee-deep in a swamp in the depths of the Bolivian jungle, hunting for anacondas in a pair of sandals, it occurred to George that perhaps he should have booked that all-inclusive honeymoon to the Maldives after all.

Join George and Rachel on their hilarious journey through the wilds of Ecuador, Peru and Bolivia, as they climb volcanoes, fish for piranhas, trek through the Amazon rainforest, take death-defying bus rides, sample some of the continent's strangest delicacies, and try to get to Machu Picchu.

Armed only with a basic knowledge of Spanish, small backpacks, and bags of enthusiasm, they set off together on what promised to be a life-changing adventure.

DID NOT FINISH:
Misadventures in Running, Cycling and Swimming

Is running a marathon with your partner a wise idea?

What about taking part in a triathlon together?

George is about to find out as he and his wife Rachel put their marriage to the test.

Now settled into life in Devon with their three children, they try to encourage a more active family lifestyle with camping holidays, family bike rides, hill-walking and canoe trips. But things rarely go smoothly.

Meanwhile, George continues to set himself ridiculous challenges. Having been a complete novice swimmer only a year earlier, he decides to confront his incompetence head-on. By signing up for a 10km swim. How hard can it be?

Did Not Finish is a series of books about George and his family's adventures in running, cycling and swimming. From ultramarathons to triathlons, 10k swims to European cycling adventures, George promises fun and laughter every step, pedal, and paddle of the way.

HOW NOT TO GET MARRIED:
Confessions of a Wedding Photographer

Before becoming an author, George Mahood spent a decade working as a wedding photographer, covering over 250 weddings. In his tongue-in-cheek memoir, he lifts the lid on the industry and the traditions and trends associated with the modern wedding.

Sometimes controversial, often insightful, but always amusing, George Mahood offers some practical advice to those planning their own wedding, sharing stories of the weddings he photographed as well as his own marriage, while shedding some light on the role of the wedding photographer and what it is like to document the most important day in these couples' lives.

Acknowledgements

Thank you to Rachel, Layla, Leo and Kitty for always putting up with me - but particularly through this holiday challenge.

Special thanks to Mum, Dad, Rachel, Miriam and Zoe Marr for their help with the editing and kind words of encouragement.

Huge thanks also to those responsible for running the holiday listing sites. In particular: Chase's Calendar of Events, Brownielocks and Holiday Insights

I would also like to reiterate my thanks to all of the amazing people who created these weird and wonderful holidays in the first place. Thank you for believing in your celebration enough to make a day out of it, and I hope that my books have helped spread the word about your special days a little further.

Thank you all again.

BIG love,
George

www.facebook.com/georgemahood
www.instagram.com/georgemahood
www.twitter.com/georgemahood
www.georgemahood.com

Made in the USA
Middletown, DE
21 August 2023

37084695R00170